A Ryan Carter Mystery

Lost Treasures of World War II

The Final Report of Karl Altman

Stephen L. Wynn

D1704758

PITTSBURGH, PENNSYLVANIA 15238

The contents of this work, including, but not limited to, the accuracy of events, people, and places depicted; opinions expressed; permission to use previously published materials included; and any advice given or actions advocated are solely the responsibility of the author, who assumes all liability for said work and indemnifies the publisher against any claims stemming from publication of the work.

All Rights Reserved
Copyright © 2024 by Stephen L. Wynn

No part of this book may be reproduced or transmitted, downloaded, distributed, reverse engineered, or stored in or introduced into any information storage and retrieval system, in any form or by any means, including photocopying and recording, whether electronic or mechanical, now known or hereinafter invented without permission in writing from the publisher.

RoseDog Books
585 Alpha Drive, Suite 103
Pittsburgh, PA 15238
Visit our website at www.rosedogbookstore.com

ISBN: 979-8-89211-054-9
eISBN: 979-8-89211-552-0

Table of Contents

Dedication v

Acknowledgment vii

About the Author ix

Newspaper Headlines from 1994 xi

Preface xiii

Day One, Wednesday February 2nd 1

Day Two, Friday February 18th 9

Day Three, Saturday February 19th 17

Day Four, Sunday February 20th 41

Day Five, Monday February 21st 69

Saying our Goodbyes .75

To my brother Jon, who taught me so many things in life.
You left too suddenly and too early. You are missed.

Acknowledgment

I need to give my deepest thanks to Christine, who graciously makes herself available 24/7 as my editor, proofreader, and IT person. She always gives me honest and sound advice and has always been very supportive of my weak and limited attempts at writing.

What you are about to read is pure fiction, a product of my imagination. All characters, incidents, and situations in this book are imaginary and have no connection to any one person or actual happening. My intent is not to insult, harm, or be disrespectful to anyone.

I hope you enjoy reading this book.

Stephen L. Wynn

About the Author

Stephen L. Wynn is retired and lives in Chisago City, Minnesota. During the summer months, he enjoys being outdoors and working in his large garden, and during the winter months, which some years can be nine months long,…..well…..he gains weight from eating too many hot dishes and pizzas and gets depressed from the cold, snow, and from watching the Minnesota Vikings, and sometimes, wonders why he lives in Minnesota. He is also the author of "The Colvers Report", which is the first book of his Ryan Carter mystery series.

Newspaper headlines you could have read in 1994

On January 6th, Olympic figure skater Nancy Kerrigan is attacked by Tanya Harding at Cobo Sports Arena in Detroit, Michigan.

On January 30th, Super Bowl # 28, the Dallas Cowboys defeated the Buffalo Bills 30 to 13.

On February 2nd, The body of former German World War II convicted war criminal Karl Altman, is discovered in an unmarked grave at an Indian Reservation in Isleta, Texas.

On March 4th, John Candy died of a heart attack, he was 43 years old.

On March 7th, The first group of women in the US Navy is assigned to the USS Eisenhower.

On April 22nd, Richard M. Nixon, 37th President, died of a stroke, he was 81 years old.

On May 13th, Johnny Carson made his last television appearance on the Late Show with David Letterman.

On May 19th, Jacqueline Kennedy Onassis died from non-Hodgkin's Lymphoma, she was 64 years old.

On June 6th, The 50th anniversary of the D-Day invasion of Normandy.

On June 17th, 95 million viewers watched OJ Simpson drive along the Los Angeles freeway fleeing police, and is later arrested for killing his wife, Nicole Brown Simpson, and Ronald Goldman.

On August 16th, The IBM Simon Personal Communicator, also known as the first Smart Phone, goes on sale.

On October 20th, Burt Lancaster died of a heart attack. He was 80 years old.

Preface

Lost Treasures of World War II, The Final Report on Karl Altman

What you are about to read is an accumulation of over forty years of information all gathered on one Karl Altman by British Intelligence MI6, the Holy Vatican, Governments of Germany, Israel, France, and Spain along with thousands of reports from the United States FBI. And who is Karl Altman you ask? Well, European historians will tell you that he was a famous art and jewel thief, known for his exquisite taste in pearls, diamonds, and priceless art, who also created a myth of a Prince of Thieves persona of himself. He is suspected of stealing over a billion dollars in gold and priceless art in today's dollars. To the European World War II War Crimes Commission, (WCC), he was a criminal who was convicted of war crimes at the Nuremberg War Trials. It has been said that he was a member of Adolph Hitler's inner circle between 1934 to 1945. And yet to some, he was one of World War II's biggest heroes, a modern-day Robin Hood who helped thousands of families survive and escape Germany during the war. A substantial difference of opinions you could say, but truth be told we just don't know who Karl Altman actually was. He definitely was a man of mystery. Our first documented record of Karl Altman was when he showed up at an Adolph Hitler political rally in the early 1930s and joined the Nazi Nationalist Party. And as fast as he arrived on the scene in 1930, he left just as fast when Allied forces advanced into Berlin to bring World War II to an end in 1945. Groups of Nazi hunters, led by the Simon Wiesenthal Center, which to this day is still following leads on all convicted Nazi war criminals, are convinced that in 1945, Karl Altman fled to either Argentina or Spain, where for 49 years he lived under a new identity and has not been seen or heard from since. That was until February 2, 1994, when Karl Altman's body was discovered in an unmarked grave, at a construction site at the Apache / Tiwa Indian Reservation in the tiny and unassuming town of Isleta, Texas.

Ryan Carter, formally of the El Paso Sheriff's Department, and now a newly appointed Special Agent with the FBI International War Crimes Division is assigned to this case, not only for his investigation skills but also for his ties to the Apache / Tiwa Indian Reservation and knowledge of their tribal laws. Ryan's mother was Apache, and he grew up on this very reservation, leaving when he was eighteen years old. His new assignment is to find out how a wanted World War II war criminal's body can turn up in the middle of an ancient Indian burial grounds 49 years after he disappeared. But first, the State Department must work out a peaceful truce and agree to special terms from the Tribal Leaders of the Apache / Tiwa Reservation before the FBI is even allowed onto the reservation. And to make this even more interesting, just as Carter is starting his investigation, the State Department informs him that he is to meet with agents from MI6 British Intelligence and Italy's Vatican Papal Police Department who have important, never seen before, Top Secret information on one Karl Altman, along with information on a 50-year-old unsolved and never reported to the public theft of one of the Vatican's most treasured possessions that they feel is important as to why Karl Altman's body was found here in Isleta, Texas.

For five days you will be sitting with Ryan Carter as he gathers information on Karl Altman that goes as far back as 1930, leaving Ryan Carter to say, "WTF, you just can't make this story up." Also from Carter's investigation, you will read about the Isleta Indian Mission, which is the oldest Mission and Church in the State of Texas that goes back to the early 1700's. You will read pre-World War II conversations from the British Royal family. You will read multiple daily journals starting in 1930 and going through 1945 from both the Vatican and Pope Pius XII. You will read about a real-life modern-day Robin Hood thief who helped thousands of families escape Germany during the war. You will see and feel the love one man had for his country that was so strong he was willing to die for it.

Day 1: Wednesday, February 2, 1994

Finding the Body of Karl Altman

"When you were born you cried, and the world rejoiced. Live your life so that when you die, the world will cry, and you will rejoice."

Cherokee Tribal saying

This story begins on February 2, 1994, at The Apache / Tiwa Indian Reservation in Isleta, Texas, which sits on twenty-three thousand acres of land on the far western side of the State of Texas. Records show the original land decree came from King Philip V of Spain in 1702 when Spain owned all rights to this land. The widest part of the reservation is just sixty-seven miles with the Rio Grande River running through most of the reservation. It is one hundred and fifty-four miles long and the town of El Paso, Texas is just three miles from the furthest, northern point of the reservation. The Tiwa community, also known as Tigua, are predominantly nonviolent farmers, growing corn, beans, and various melons. They are also famously known for their pottery. The Apache community is known for their hunting skills and for being great warriors and protectors.

For survival, the two tribes formed an allegiance that goes back to the late 1700's and has coexisted to this day. Officially, the Apache community sits in the northern portion of the reservation, while the Tiwa community sits in the southern portion of the reservation. There is an elected governing body of twelve tribal leaders, consisting of six Apache and six Tiwa members, with approximately twenty-seven hundred total members on the reservation. They have their own police force and are legally considered, like all Indian reservations, a country within the United States. The historical Ysleta Mission, which serves as the main entrance to the reservation, also provides a church and school for the reservation and is recognized as the oldest, continuously operated religious mission in the State of Texas. The church is operated by the order of Jesuits priests and the school is staffed with four local lay teachers and six Nuns from the order of Sisters of Charity of the Incarnate World. Sitting just four hundred yards south of the mission is the small town of Isleta, Texas, which consists of a general store (that also serves as the Town Hall and Court House), three cafe's, four cantinas, a gas station, a Doctor and Veterinarians office, and approximately forty homes, with maybe twenty being usable. All of this is on the only road in and out of the reservation and is called Red Fox Road.

Most days you will find droves of tents scattered around town with craftsmen selling their pottery and miscellaneous Indian artifacts to the over one hundred thousand tourists that will visit the mission and town each year. Today was to be a larger than normal day for tourists, with the start of the eight-day celebration of the Powamu Festival, where it is said that deceased family ancestral spirits will visit the communities to bring good health and rain for their upcoming planting season. To the tribal leaders and all of the members of the community, it was going to be a huge, festive day on the reservation. Starting in the morning with a mass at the church, followed by traditional Apache and Tiwa tribal dancing by students from the school and speeches by tribal leaders.

Today was also the day the two communities were going to do something that had not been attempted or even considered in almost fifty years, and that was to start the construction of two new buildings just east of the Mission that will house the Apache / Tiwa Tribal Cultural Center and the Apache / Tiwa Tribal Government Offices. The last time any construction was attempted at the mission was in 1946 when seven Jesuit missionaries came from Leon, Spain on a pilgrimage and stayed at the Mission for one year and did repairs to the Church and school and built a new barn for the animals. Today, architects and construction crews that have experience in restoring and building adobe buildings were to make years of hard work and dreams of the Tribal Leaders and members of the reservation of both communities come true. The mayors of Mexico City and El Paso, Texas, along with US Congressman Elrondo Cruz of Texas, and the Honorable Hector Alverez, the Mayor of Isleta, Texas, were all on hand to celebrate the special day.

However, about an hour after the construction crews started excavating at the new building site, they were surprised when they uncovered human bones. After hours of careful digging by hand, it was determined that they had found an ancient Indian burial site, causing all festivities of the day to come to an end. For the next ten days, community leaders, community members, and the construction crew continued digging by hand an area of twenty feet by twenty feet and roughly five feet deep and uncovered thirty-six skeletons. Some of the skeletons looked like they could go back hundreds of years by the special ornamental beads, spears, and buffalo robes and were thought to be from the Tiwa community.

Now, some Indian communities build burial platforms above ground for their deceased so the spirit can travel to the afterlife, but the Tiwa community bury their deceased just below the surface of the ground, with the belief that the body of the deceased will strengthen the mother earth that the community rests on. It was agreed by the Elders that this was indeed a grave site of deceased Tiwa Elders, and this unmarked burial ground was a mystery to all of them.

Burial grounds are very sacred in all Indian communities, and for the Tiwa Indian community to not be aware of this burial site caused a huge embarrassment to the Tiwa Tribal Leaders and created distrust in leadership among the tribal members. The Tiwa Tribal Shaman or Holy Man was summoned, and he declared this newfound burial site as hallowed grounds that should never be disturbed, causing any future thoughts of construction on this site to come to a halt. But if that didn't put enough of a damper on the day, upon further examination of the burial site, another body was discovered which was noticeably different from the other bodies.

It was evident that this newfound body was just thrown into a much shallower grave. The body was lying on its side, with its legs twisted like it was running, with one arm beneath the body and the other arm extended like it was trying to cover its head. They could tell the deceased was Caucasian and not from the Indian community, but possibly of a religious community, because they could still make out small pieces of wool-like fabric, like that of a robe with a hood on the body, like what Monks or Missionaries would wear. They could also tell the body had not been buried in the grave for as long as the other bodies. A quick guess by Doctor Linius Ockermeyer, Isleta's medical Doctor, Undertaker, and Veterinarian, is that the body was a male, maybe in his 70s or 80s, and giving a rough estimate that the body was thrown into this grave about twenty years ago, making it about 1975. A leather briefcase could also be seen under the body. Upon further investigation, Doctor Ockermeyer stated that this body also had one big distinctive difference from the other bodies in the grave site which was, this body had a bullet hole in the back of its head.

Melvin Crowman of the Apache community and Chief of the Joint Tribal Police Department knew that his small tribal police department was not equipped to handle this investigation, so he was forced to call the El Paso Sheriff's Department. Once that call was made, it took less than an hour for the El Paso Sheriff's homicide and forensic teams to be on site. They recovered, among other things, teeth and strands of hair from the deceased and two sets of fingerprints from the briefcase, which they sent to the Regional FBI office in El Paso, Texas, where they then ran the necessary tests for identification, and after finding no hits on their FBI database, they immediately sent all the information to local and state agencies, and after receiving no results from them, the information was then loaded into the Interpol Watch list, which immediately triggered a hit on the identification of the deceased.

The body was identified as one Karl Altman, a World War II convicted war criminal, and even though he was never captured or arrested by the Allied forces, he was still tried and found guilty in 1945 at the Allied Nuremberg War Trials for war crimes of murdering thousands of Jewish and Russian civilians and stealing millions of dollars of priceless art and artifacts that have never been recovered. Since 1945, British Intelligence and groups of Nazi War Hunters, led by the Simon Wiesenthal Center, have been following leads that have Karl Altman either fleeing to Argentina or Spain after Germany's surrender. Wherever he went has always been a mystery. That was until today, February 2nd, 1994.

Within five hours of the discovery and identification of the body, an Urgent Top-Secret bulletin was issued to the President's Cabinet Members; Marleen O'Sullivan, the Director of the U.S. Interior, Alberto Juanrez, the Director of the Bureau of Indian Affairs and Clearance Kellerman, the Director of the FBI, along with phone calls across the Atlantic Ocean to agencies in Germany, Poland, Great Britain, and Israel describing the discovery and identification of convicted war criminal Karl Altman, with all of them claiming they wanted ownership rights of the body and leadership of the case. The President of the United States listened to everyone plead their case of why they should be given the lead in this case, and after engaging in long and sometimes heated discussions, the President felt there was only one man qualified who could be trusted to oversee this potentially explosive and sensitive situation that could become an international nightmare. The President reached for his private phone and called his friend, Assistant U.S. Attorney General Joseph Friedman.

The President knew the first problem Friedman would have to overcome was to bridge the political and social differences between the Apache / Tiwa communities and the U.S. Government. The second problem would be dealing with Germany, Poland, Great Britain, Italy, Israel, and the Jewish Institutions, all wanting to have their representatives involved with or leading the investigation. According to all of them, Karl Altman was a convicted war criminal for crimes committed in Europe and each demanded they should have the lead in this case. Diplomacy was going to be the key to dealing with all these European Presidents and the Apache / Tiwa Tribal Leaders. Again, the President felt Joseph Friedman was the only man who could handle that, but the President knew his third problem was going to be the hardest. He had to convince Joseph Friedman to take the job.

Two hours later while the President was still on the phone pleading his case to Joseph Friedman, he heard of a raid by the El Paso Sheriff's Department, who stormed the main gate of the Apache / Tiwa Reservation and demanded entrance to remove the body of Karl Altman. With about thirty armed tribal members standing at the ready, it was explained to the Sheriff's deputies that because the Tribal

Shaman or Holy Man declared the grave site holy grounds, no one was allowed on the site and reminded the Sheriff's deputies that this was Apache / Tiwa Indian sovereignty, and they had no jurisdiction on the reservation. Tensions were high, to say the least, with everybody. By now local and national news agencies had picked up on the story and were all parked in the main parking lot of the reservation trying to uncover any news. All news outlets were reporting how Sheriff's deputies had stormed the main gate but were turned away by armed members of the reservation and that the Governor of Texas activated three hundred National Guard members and were having them deployed to the Reservation. The press was feverishly trying to find the story here. The Tribal Leaders had no choice but to issue a written statement that until further notice the main gate onto the reservation would be closed. Only community members would be allowed to enter. The President was watching all of this on his television as he was talking, this was what he didn't want to happen and said so to Joseph Friedman, who was still respectfully refusing to be involved. But after another thirty minutes of back-and-forth yelling and laughing, an agreement was made, and two hours later Joseph Friedman was on an airplane to El Paso, Texas, and then a one-hour drive to the Apache / Tiwa Indian Reservation.

 The first thing Joseph Friedman did was to set up a meeting with the Tribal Leaders, and after spending two days of back-and-forth negotiating, an agreement was reached with four conditions. The first condition agreed upon was The Apache /Tiwa Indian Community would receive their 8.3 million-dollar (plus interest) 1864 Relocation Settlement that was awarded to the Community in U.S. District Court six years ago, that had yet to be released by the Bureau of Indian Affairs and its Director Alberto Juanrez. The second condition was that only two agents or government representatives would be allowed on the reservation during the investigation of the murder of

Karl Altman, and once they arrived, they would not be allowed to leave the reservation until the case was completed and they would be under the supervision of Senior Tribal Leader Joseph Redhorse and Tribal Police Chief Melvin Crowman. The third condition was they would not be allowed to disturb or take any pictures of the other thirty-six skeletons. Friedman stressed that the grave site where the body of Karl Altman was found was a crime scene and some pictures and testing would be needed for forensic testing. He stressed to them that they would be respectful of the deceased. Tribal Leaders agreed to that. The fourth and final condition was that the investigation must be completed in five days, after which the body of Karl Altman would then be allowed to be removed from the reservation. U.S. Assistant Attorney General Joseph Friedman, speaking for the President, agreed to all four conditions immediately. He looked at Director Alberto Juanrez and instructed him to have the check released immediately and for Juanrez to hand deliver the check by the end of the business day tomorrow. Friedman then informed the Tribal Council that he would prepare a signed agreement with the four conditions agreed upon and would have it delivered to the Tribal Council by the end of business today. He stood up, shook everyone's hands, and walked out of the room. He did not stick around for any small talk because he had work to do. He knew he had to make phone calls to calm down the leaders of the European countries and tell them they would not be involved in this case, and then he had to find two people who could handle this investigation without causing a world incident. He knew who he wanted, but like him, it might be difficult to convince them that they wanted to do it.

Day 2: Friday, February 18, 1994

Creating the Investigative Team

"Our lives are fashioned by our choices. First, we make our choices, then our choices make us."
Anne Frank

U.S. Marshals Office, El Paso Texas, February 18, 1994, 4:10 pm
My name is Ryan Carter, and I work in the El Paso County Courthouse as a Deputy U.S. Marshal. Today is my last day of work before I go on my approved and much-needed three-week vacation. According to the DOJ personnel handbook, my workday ends at 4:30, and according to the clock on the wall, I still had 20 minutes left to work. I was trying to act like I was busy doing paperwork etc., but I was really just passing the time till my vacation started. It's been seventeen months, thirteen days, and seven and a half hours since my last vacation, but who's counting right?

A lot has happened since my last vacation. First, I received a promotion, well actually all they did was slide my desk from being next to the bathroom door, to now I sit next to a window that overlooks the parking lot and the garbage dumpsters in the back of the building.

The promotion also gave me more work to do. I now supervise ten other deputies and two secretaries, and oh yes, they did not increase my salary because of the federal wage freeze that was in effect then and still is now.

Besides the great views and smells I get from my window each day, I also get to look directly into the office of my boss, Deputy Director John Galone, and at the moment, I could see he was talking on the telephone and looking right at me. I saw him shake his head and wave his arms kind of like in protest to the person he was talking to. I looked at the clock on the wall above the doorway and I could see I still had 10 minutes left until my workday would end and my vacation would start. I watched as the Director hung up his phone, stood up, and stretched. He then started shuffling papers on his desk like he was looking for a particular paper, he then suddenly looked up and at that moment we both made and held eye contact. I watched as he walked around his desk, and while still looking at me, he started walking toward me. I looked at the clock again and continued doing my countdown, which was at 9 minutes and counting.

As he walked out of his office and walked towards my desk, holding a piece of paper he took from his desk in his left hand, he grabbed a chair from another desk with his right hand and dragged it behind him. My countdown was at 8 minutes by the time he set the chair in front of my desk and sat down. He never was one to make small talk, so I was surprised when he asked how I was doing and did I have any major problems today. I told him I had a busy day and that nothing big was happening in the courthouse, keeping my personal life of my planned vacation out of the conversation. He asked for, and I gave him, a verbal recap of today's arrests and the status of all active cases. He acted totally interested, even asking questions, which surprised me because not more than 30 minutes ago I gave him my DSR Report, (Daily Status Report), which gave him all this information. All of this did not go unnoticed by me, so I knew something was up and I knew he was stalling.

He leaned back in his chair and looked at me for what seemed to be an awkward and uncomfortable 20 seconds, giving me the feeling, he had something else on his mind. I looked up at the clock and did the math, I still had 7 minutes to go before my workday ends and my vacation starts. Finally, he wiggled in his chair like he was a little uncomfortable or because he was too big for the chair, which I thought might be the problem. It was no secret in the office that he loved his donuts. Leaning forward he placed his elbows on my desk and looked right at me and said, "So have you heard the latest news?" When I told him I didn't know what he meant, he proceeded to tell me about the discovery of the body of one Karl Altman, a big-time World War II convicted war criminal from Nazi Germany who went missing in 1945. T minus 6 minutes to go I said to myself. He started to give me a history lesson about Karl Altman and World War II, finally telling me how Altman's body was found in an unmarked burial site at the Apache / Tiwa Indian Reservation. "Just ten miles from here," he said with a little enthusiasm in his voice, as he pointed out my window in the direction of where the Indian Reservation was. He then proceeded to tell me how for the past two days, the Government had been trying to come to an agreement with the Tribal Leaders so they could remove the body. I knew of the huge distrust the Indian community had with the U.S. Government. "Good luck with that", I said out loud.

Flashing my eyes to the clock I saw it was down to T minus 5 minutes to go. I was thinking to myself that Deputy Director John Galone knew I was familiar with the reservation, because he knew that my mother was an Apache Indian, a daughter of a former Tribal Leader, and he also knew I was born on the reservation, spending the first 17 years of my life at the mission and still having some family members and close friends living there. He also knew that after my grandfather died, my mother was banished from the community because she had married my father, a white man. Today, for an Apache woman to marry a white man is not a big deal and is somewhat accepted by the younger generation, but back in the 60's it was unheard of, but because my grandfather was an elder Tribal Leader, the community looked the other way until his death.

T minus 4 minutes to go. I noticed that the Director had also been looking up at the clock and it was at that moment that I knew I was not going to like what was going to happen next. Deputy Director John Galone stood up and I heard him say 'I'm sorry Ryan." Then he set the piece of paper that he had in his hands in front of me and, taking a deep breath, told me my vacation was canceled and that I've been immediately re-assigned. He then turned around and quickly walked back to his office and closed his door. I looked down and grabbed the paper and read it, and I could not believe this was happening. Now when I looked up at the clock it finally said 4:30.

So not only was I not going on vacation, but according to this piece of paper, I was working tomorrow and would be temporarily living on the reservation, which would force me to relive and confront my family heritage. That's how my day ended. I reread the paper again to make sure I wasn't dreaming...... I wasn't.

From: The President of the United States of America
To: Deputy United States Marshal Ryan Carter, E.N. C3321189
Date: Friday, February 18, 1994, 3:10 pm
Highly Sensitive Materials.

By order of the President of the United States, and by special order code FS 311-7, this is to notify you that as of today's date, February 18, 1994, you are assigned, TAD to the Department of Justice, Bureau of Investigations (FBI), the Office of Special Investigations Division, (OSI), where you will report directly to U.S. Assistant Attorney General Joseph Friedman until further notice.

It is also ordered that you will immediately proceed to the Tribal Police Station, located at the main entry gate of the Apache / Tiwa Indian Reservation, at 13345 South Red Fox Road, in Isleta, Texas by 0700 hours on Saturday, February 19, 1994, where you will receive further instructions. It is further ordered that during your investigation, you and your team will be required to abide by all laws and customs of the Apache / Tiwa Indian Community and that said community is requiring you to stay on said reservation during this investigation for a term not to exceed (5) five days.
s/s William Jefferson Clinton, President.
CC : DOJ, USAG Joseph Friedman
Page 1 of 1

Southern Methodist University, Dallas, Texas - February 18, 1994, 4:45 pm
Walking out to her car, 38-year-old Anna Marie Friedman, an Associate Professor at Southern Methodist University, heard her name being yelled. Looking over her shoulder she saw a man running towards her waving his arms for her to stop. He looked too old to be a student she told herself. As he was getting closer she could see he was wearing a suit and tie with a tan overcoat, definitely not a student she thought. He ran up and stopped in front of her with a slight smile on his face and immediately proceeded to bend over and placed his hands on his knees, trying to talk while struggling to catch his breath, she heard him say he was "Philip Harrison, Personal Assistant to U.S. Assistant Attorney General Joseph Friedman, who is asking for 15

minutes of your time." Anna felt sorry for Philip, having to serve as an errand boy for the all-mighty Joseph Friedman, her father. Anna wondered if Philip knew she was Joseph Friedman's daughter. "Tell him I'm not interested and for him to call my office to make an appointment", Anna replied and started to turn and continue walking to her car. "Ma'am, if I can be more direct," Phillip said, still trying to catch his breath. "He said you might say something like that, but my orders are to take you back to the car walking with you or carrying you," he said while trying to make a stern and mean look on his chubby baby face. I have to say I respected Philips's determination on following orders, and I was thinking he knew I could level him with one punch if I wanted to force the issue. Looking at him I kind of felt sorry for him, I'm sure he was in his last year of law school and this was an internship job, and he didn't want to be on the bad side of U.S. Assistant Attorney General Joseph Friedman. Now my father and I are not very close. We used to be, but ever since my mother and sister died, we just drifted apart. We both buried ourselves in our work. He dove into his work at the State Department and I spent eighteen months working with Doctor Simon Goldberg at the War Museum of Sire in Israel, then went on to complete my Doctorate degree at John Hopkins University, and a year later I was fortunate enough to be hired as an associate professor at Southern Methodist University teaching European History which included historical figures such as Napoleon Bonaparte, Karl Marx, and Adolph Hitler to the young and hungry students who knew next to nothing about European history and it's culture, especially the hardships of the German, Polish and Jewish people during the World War II years.

 As I stood looking at Philip Harrison, I asked myself, what could be so damn important that Joseph Friedman would have his Personal Assistant run me down and make demands that I meet him at his car immediately. I was curious to find out so I said, "Okay Phillip lets you and I walk back to the car and see what the old man wants," I said with a smile. Philip gave me a bigger smile back and said, "Thank you." I think Phillip knew he was in trouble if he had to force the issue. It took us almost fifteen minutes to walk to my father's car, which was in the main parking lot on the other side of the campus, but the walk gave us time to get acquainted and time for me to think of my father. I have to admit I've missed my father and there was a part of me excited about seeing him. As we came up to the parking lot, I saw him standing next to his car, wearing an all-too-familiar dark suit, looking tall and thin, he looked great. I found myself running up to him to give him a big hug. This feels good, I said to myself. Holding him I could smell that Old Spice after-shave lotion he always wore. I could feel the strength in his arms. We both stood looking at each other through moistened eyes and neither one of us knew what to say. Finally, I saw him point and say, "Let's go sit on the park bench and talk." We spent the next fifteen minutes or so telling each other how good each of us looked. Then me telling him about my job at the University, and he told me he still works too hard and knows he needs to slow down. Finally, he looked at me and said, "I need help, you're the only one I could think of."

He proceeded to tell me about the finding of a body of a World War II war criminal in a 300-year-old Indian burial grounds right here in Texas. As soon as he said war criminal from World War II, I held up my hands and told him I wanted in. He smiled and said, "Great, you start tomorrow, now let me fill you in with the information that I have."

Day 3: Saturday, February 19, 1994

Arriving at the Main Gate at the Reservation

"Life is like riding a bicycle: to keep your balance you must keep moving."

Albert Einstein

The sun was just starting to rise in the east allowing me to see the multiple shades of brown and red on the desert horizon. I could just make out the tips of the Franklin Mountains that were starting to peek through the blanket of darkness. The air had a clean, fresh, and somewhat damp smell to it. Like every morning, there was no wind to speak of, and it was always guaranteed that every day was going to be hot and sunny in Isleta, Texas. Giving us another day that we will live up to our nickname " Sun City". As I turned left off Santiago Creek Road onto the hilly, dusty, and very bumpy dirt road known as South Red Fox Road, I was still not in the best of moods and was thinking about the events of the last twenty-four hours. I was wishing the Director was sitting next to me in the car, so I could tell him how I had been looking forward to my vacation, and how I really wasn't looking forward to being on the reservation again, but the more I thought of everything I think he knew that, so I tried to calm myself down and said this assignment must be important. I looked down at my speedometer and was surprised I was going ninety miles an hour. I slowed down, I had to snap out of this funky mood. So, I started thinking of the hundreds of times I drove down this dirt road as a kid. The Apache / Tiwa Indian Communities allow fourteen-year-olds to drive on the reservation, but my uncle Reymond started letting me drive when I was twelve. I was big for my age, so I always looked older than I actually was.

Uncle Reymond and I would drive to the junkyard in El Paso in his old beat-up Ford pickup truck loaded with scrap metal, three times a week. He would pick me up at my house and with my mother waving goodbye to us, he would drive just far enough down the road so she could not see us anymore, where he would stop the truck and tell me to drive, which would then allow Uncle Reymond to fall asleep or pass out while leaning on the passenger door. Many times, that door would fly open while I was driving, and I would have to lean over and grab him before he would fall out. He was always too drunk to remember any of it. I would drive down this road going eighty-plus miles an hour with the radio blasting, many times losing most of our scrap metal as it flew out of the truck going over these potholes.

After we dropped our scrap metal off, Uncle Reymond would buy four cases of beer, which he would drink almost one case on the way home, a candy bar for me, and he would always buy something for my mother. I shared many laughs with old Uncle Reymond. He made sure I went to school every day and would buy me new school clothes every year. He was from the Apache community, and he taught me how to fight, hunt, and fish. He always was there for my mother, who was his sister. He died when I was fifteen. I miss him.

I finally arrived at the main gate of the Apache / Tiwa Indian Reservation, which forced me to leave my happy thoughts of Uncle Reymond as I slowly drove up to the security guard who was standing with his hand held up for me to stop. After showing him my credentials and signing in on the entry log, I continued into the parking lot. There was not a tree, a bush, or anything green in my eyesight. This was the start of the Chihuahua Desert I said to myself. Maybe I was used to the desert when I lived here as a kid, but now that I've been gone for over ten years it was kind of eerie and almost frightening.

I could tell there hadn't been any upgrades to the entrance or the parking lot since I left. The same huge boulders that were scattered around the four sides of the parking lot ten years ago, were still there. And then there was the run-down-looking Tribal police shack. As a kid, I was told the building was over eighty- years old. To me, I always called it our Statue of Liberty, because whenever I drove onto the reservation and I saw that building I knew I was home, and I was safe. Unfortunately, what I called the Statue of Liberty, most of the tribal members referred to it as the outhouse because that's what it looked like. It has always looked like it needed a coat of paint because of the sun beating on it all day. Inside I knew there would be two small tables with four chairs and one cell, which the door didn't lock. The year I turned sixteen I worked for the Reservation Police Department as a guard and worked many shifts in that building. Even back then I knew I wanted to go into police work. I never would have thought I would say this, but I miss those days.

When I drove into the parking lot, I was amazed to see it already full of vehicles. Years ago, there might have been three cars parked overnight in it, with two of those cars having the owners sleeping in them because they came home drunk, but this morning was different. Finding a dead body on the reservation will surely change the norm at an Indian reservation I thought. Looking at the skyline, I could see the sun was just starting to peek over the horizon. telling me it was about 6:15 or 6:20, and I could already feel the heat. I parked my car so I could watch all the comings and goings in the parking lot. I could see at least ten trucks from both national and local television and radio stations along with maybe twenty trucks from the Army National Guard, all parked in three neat rows in the field on the far side of the parking lot. Next to the trucks were four tents, I'm thinking living quarters for the troops. There was also a large, tall tent that had no sides on it, allowing me to see tables and chairs inside the tent. I assumed that would be the main command center if it were needed. Next to the tents, I saw two large mobile homes with black iron rail steps to the doors. There were two squad cars from the Reservation Police Department and three black Suburban's parked in front of the trailers which I was sure belonged to the FBI or some other DOJ agency. I knew there was no love between the Apache / Tiwa Indian Communities and the U.S. Government, especially the FBI, so having all these Suburban's and Army National Guard vehicles around was telling me the negotiations between the government and tribal leaders had not gone well for the FBI.

Sitting in my car, with the rising sun shining on me through the windshield was making me relaxed and sleepy after my early drive here. I closed my eyes and went down memory lane again. I reminded myself that on March 3rd, it would be nine years since I last drove past that guard shack onto the reservation for my mother's funeral. I haven't been back since that day. I know to some that would make me a terrible son, but Apaches deal with a loved one's death and funeral differently than white people. I can still hear the chanting from the Shaman and the people of the community as they stood with me for two days and nights singing the death songs and praying for her trip into the next world. Apaches believe that loved ones must be buried, so their spirit can be free to be with their ancestors. It is also an Apache tradition that the deceased's home and all their possessions be burned, so evil spirits can't attach to them and haunt the remaining family. I miss my mother immensely, and my heart aches to have just one more talk with her, but I know she is in a better place than this Apache / Tiwa Reservation. I know she is always with me in spirit. When I was living on the reservation, I wasn't very popular with the older members because I was half white, and after my grandfather died, they made it very hard on me and my mother and after the funeral, I vowed I would never set foot again on this reservation.

Suddenly I was shaken from my dream by the arrival of two black Chevy Suburban's as they raced into the parking lot. They caused a huge cloud of dust and came to a sliding stop maybe ten feet from the guard shack. I knew they were not members of the reservation, it's unwritten rule in the community that you drive slowly in the parking lot and on all roads, so as to not raise dust. It's just called being considerate. I watched as two men and a woman got out of the first vehicle and four men got out of the second vehicle, all standing around their vehicles and acting like they were waiting for someone. I was wondering why they were here. I crawled out of my car and gave a loud moan as I stretched and tried to wake up. I noticed they all looked over at me. I walked to the back of my car opened the trunk and placed my gun and badge inside and made sure all doors were locked. I was dressed in an old pair of blue jeans and an old work shirt topped off with an old cowboy hat. I thought it was best that I dress as the local members did, and besides, wearing a suit and tie just made me hot thinking about it.

As I started walking towards the guard shack, I could see that all the men were dressed in dark blue suits, and all had aviator sunglasses on, I noticed the woman was wearing a pair of old faded blue jeans with a light green shirt and a Dallas Cowboys baseball cap. A nice touch I thought, seeing that I'm a huge Dallas Cowboys fan. She looked to be about thirty to thirty-five years old, standing maybe five feet ten inches, definitely under a hundred and twenty pounds I guessed with blond hair that was tied back in a short ponytail. She looked nervous or excited, as she kept looking around as if she was looking for someone.

All this I noticed as I was walking toward the guard shack when suddenly one of the FBI agents yelled and walked up and stood in front of me, and in a loud stern voice told me to stop, turn around and go back to my car. He said it loud enough that all the agents turned to give me a once-over look and judged me that I was not a threat to them, so they all turned back and continued their conversations among themselves, leaving this one agent to deal with me. Standing where I was, I could hear the popping sounds coming from the hot engines of their vehicles. They must have driven from far away I thought. Finally, because I hadn't moved or said anything yet, two other agents broke away from their conversations and walked up to me and again told me to go back to my car, while causally pulling back their suit coats and exposing their badges and weapons on their belts.

Being the smart ass that I am, I told them that "Only Indians with bloodshot eyes were allowed to carry weapons on the reservations. You don't look Indian or have red bloodshot eyes," I extended my left hand and said, "So hand me your weapons or I will have to arrest you." I heard someone laugh and then the remaining agents started walking toward me, I'm sure they were thinking that I was a drunk troublemaker Indian. Suddenly I raised my hands and said, "Or give me a bottle of whiskey and I will let you all pass," acting like I was indeed drunk. They all started laughing and the biggest one, whom I heard one of the other agents refer to him as Moose, started yelling as he walked up to me and called me a no-good worthless drunken piss-ant Indian. He started to grab for me, but before his fingers could touch my shirt, using my left hand, I grabbed his wrist while bending it backward and with my right hand, I reached out and pulled his pistol out of its holster and pressed it to his forehead between his eyes, all the while bending his wrist and forcing him to his knees. It happened so fast that it took a while before anyone realized what had just happened. Just then the door of one of the RV trailers opened and Police Chief Melvin Crowman walked out along with another man whom I recognized as Assistant Attorney General Joseph Friedman. Behind me, I heard the woman from the Suburban call out "Daddy" and then run up to give Joseph Friedman a big hug. Police Chief Melvin Crowman started walking towards me with a huge smile on his face, all the while I was still holding the gun to the FBI agent known as Moose. "All of you, stand down" he yelled while looking at the agents and me. There was a deafening silence in the air. The birds were even silent as if they didn't want to miss any of the excitement. The only sound that could be heard was the heavy breathing coming from Moose and the shuffling of boots from Police Chief Melvin Crowman, as he walked up and stood in front of me and Agent "Moose". You could have cut the tension in the air with a knife as the rest of the agents watched, wondering what they should do. "I see I have taught you well Agent Ryan, but for now please let this white piece of trash up so we can deal with the more pressing problems that we have." I looked around at the other agents, I could tell they were willing to go to war to protect their partner. I looked at Moose, sweat was dripping down his face, I'm sure having his wrist bent that far back had to be painful and he knew just a little twitch from me, and his wrist would be broken. His eyes were darting back and forth from his wrist to me. I let go of Moose's wrist and pulled the pistol back from his forehead, I ejected the shells and threw the pistol onto the ground. I noticed I left a nice little imprint of a circle on his forehead. Moose stood up slowly and started rubbing his right wrist and as he started to walk away, he said he wouldn't forget this. I gave him a little smile and in a loud enough voice for him and his partners to hear I told him he better, I could bury him in this Godforsaken desert where nobody would ever find him.

As tough as he acted, he knew I wasn't kidding. He stood there for a second, looking at me and I saw fear slowly develop in his eyes. He knew he messed with the wrong Indian. I knew I wasn't going to hear from him again. As he walked away, I shook my head realizing I hadn't been on the reservation for ten minutes and I was already calling myself an Indian, something I swore I would never do again since my mother's funeral. With Moose and his fellow agents leaving, I turned toward Chief Crowman, and with a loud laugh, he said "Ryan Carter, you haven't changed a bit!" He grabbed me and gave me a bear-like hug. "You do know how to make an entrance. It's great to see you again son."

Assistant Attorney General Joseph Friedman also walked up and said he was happy to see me again, referring to my last case just four months ago, where I worked with him in solving a wrongful death murder case. As he was shaking my hand he said he would like to introduce me to his daughter, Anna. She held out her hand for me to shake and said, "My father has spoken very highly about you, and I look forward to working with you." While shaking her hand I said, "Thank you, and your father also has also spoken highly about you and how much he loves you." Anna looked at me and started laughing and said, "I thought Indians never lied but thank you for saying that." I detected everything was not right between Anna and her father as she gave her father a strained look, then looked away. I wanted to tell her that I was only half Indian and so I was allowed to tell little white lies once in a while, but I just smiled. I heard the engines of the two black Chevy Suburbans revving up and I saw Chief Crowman walk over and start talking to the driver of the first vehicle. I don't know what was said, but they drove away like they were in a funeral, causing no dust at all.

Holding his daughter's hand, Joseph Friedman started to walk towards the trailer leaving all of us to follow. As he was about to enter the trailer he turned and said, "This will be where you will work and meet for the next week." We all walked in and stopped to take in the new digs. What I saw took me by surprise. From the outside, the trailer looked brand new, but once inside I quickly realized the trailer was stripped of all the amenities that would make this a home. All the walls were white, the floor had no carpet, just plywood, and a light bulb was hanging from wires in the middle of the living room ceiling providing just a dim circle of light to the middle of the room. Three skylights in the ceiling would provide additional light during the day. The windows all had window shades, which were all pulled down now except for the one window that had an air conditioner in it. In the desert everyone keeps their window shades closed during the day to block the hot sun from heating the home up. Except for two long white tables with six unmatched folding chairs around each, an empty easel, and a large blackboard on wheels, there was no furniture in the trailer. I noticed that one of the tables in the living room had a tall stack of folders along with three or four large rolled-up maps and a stack of yellow legal tablets and a box of government-issued pens. The kitchen was at the front of the trailer. An electric coffee pot and a stack of Styrofoam coffee cups sat on the kitchen counter. Those were the only things in the kitchen. All the comforts needed for a working office, I thought.

I noticed Friedman was standing next to the blackboard, Chief Crowman was still standing by the door, and Anna was slowly walking toward her father, as was I, when I saw the outside door open and heard Chief Crowman say "yah-ah-tay", which is a form of saying hello in the Apache and Tiwa language. There was a second or two that the sun was shining through the opening of the door and was blinding me so I couldn't make out who was coming in. I could just see the outline of a large man, and after he took a couple of steps into the trailer, I could see that it was Apache Community Leader Joseph Redhorse.

When I saw him standing there looking at me with a big smile on his ugly face, it was as if I was ten years old again. Redhorse was my youth spiritual leader when I was younger. Meaning he was the father I never had. If I had a problem, I would always go to him. He taught me the things you don't learn in school. He looked the same as he did twenty years ago. He was wearing blue jeans and a tan shirt with a leather vest that had tribal symbols on the front and back, standing about six foot three, big chested, and his hair still cut in a crew cut, still looking like the Marine that he was years ago.

I didn't hesitate, I walked up to him and gave him a big hug and told him it was great to see him again. I have to admit I could have easily broken down and cried for joy, but for not wanting to embarrass myself, I just stood there with a big smile. To see Redhorse and Chief Crowman, two men who were instrumental in my upbringing, both in one day was indeed very special to me, but I had a strange feeling about seeing both. *There is a saying in the Apache and the Tiwa language, Gitche Manitou, which in English means, beware of danger, because the Great Spirit and the creator of all things is looking at you and death is sure to follow. What was The Great Spirt trying to tell me? Was there danger and death ahead for me? Was the Great Spirit telling me something about this case?* It definitely was a sign that I had to respect.

Joseph Friedman walked over and extended his hand to Redhorse and introduced Anna, then he said he hated to break up the reunion, but we had work to do and not a lot of time. Friedman pointed towards the tables, and we all walked over and grabbed a chair, and sat down. He started the conversation by saying he was going to break us into two groups as he walked over and started writing on the blackboard. We all watched and listened as he wrote, "The first group of Ryan and Chief Crowman will revisit and review the body and crime scene." It was quite evident that penmanship was not one of his strong points. I struggled to understand what he was writing as he continued to scribble what he wanted Chief Crowman and me to do. 1)…..Confirm the identity of the body as actually one Karl Altman. 2)…. Investigate the means of his demise. 3)…. Identify the caliber of the bullet that killed him. 4)…. Review the contents of the briefcase. 5)…..Secure and review the forensic file on Karl Altman. 6)…. Take pictures of the grave site. 7)…..Create a Bio on the grave site. "What's the history of this grave site and why was it unknown to the community? I know the body has been buried here for years," he said as he turned to look at us, "But confirm what the forensic people say, and then re-confirm, see if they missed anything. We need answers." He stopped to light a cigarette, then said "These folders, as he pointed to the stack of about twenty folders on the table, is everything we have at the moment on Karl Altman, but I've requested additional information from our European allies, which they say will be here tomorrow. You call me at any time if you need anything to help expedite this case."

Next, he turned his attention to Anna and Redhorse, and again turned and started to scribble on the blackboard as he said, "The second group of Anna and Redhorse will study Karl Altman." He listed three items that he wanted them to do. 1)….Create a Bio on Karl Altman. 2)… If this is Karl Altman, where has he been since the war ended. 3)….And why was he here in Isleta, Texas? He pointed to them and said, "You will use the second table as your work area. The folders on that table should provide you with some information on Karl Altman to get you started, with more information coming tomorrow. Again, my card is on the table if you need to get ahold of me."

Freidman looked at both Anna and me and said, "You will be working separately gathering information, but each day you will meet and share all that information. Communication between the both of you will be the key to solving this case." We thought he was done and were ready to stand up and get started, but he was still looking and reading his notes all the while snuffing out his cigarette in the ashtray.

He looked at Anna and me and said, "I want to make sure you both understand that until the completion of this case, you will not be allowed to leave the reservation for any reason or communicate with anyone off the reservation about this case, do you both understand?" Anna and I both started shaking our heads and said "yes". He continued looking at us for a few seconds to ensure we both understood what he had just said. He then continued by saying "Housing has been arranged by Mr. Redhorse for both of you to stay at the mission. Both of you will always be accompanied by either Chief Crowman or Mr. Redhorse, they will drive you to and from your quarters to these trailers or anywhere else on the reservation that you might need to go for this investigation. A tribal police officer will be stationed in front of the mission at night for your protection. There are some members of this community who do not like outsiders, especially anyone with ties to the FBI. Also, the ladies of the community have volunteered to make you two meals a day to be delivered to this trailer." Finally, looking at Anna, he said in a softer voice "Remember there was a murder here, so I want you both to be careful. It's been a long day for everyone so let's stop for the day and start fresh in the morning. I will meet you here tomorrow night at 6:00 for updates."

We all stood up to leave, I grabbed about eight files that were on my table to read tonight, along with two legal tablets and a couple of pens. I noticed Anna grabbed some tablets and files from her table also.

Chief Crowman and Redhorse were busy talking to Friedman, so Anna and I walked out of the trailer. Standing in the parking lot waiting for our chauffeurs/security detail, I noticed how Anna was looking and seeing the beauty of the desert. She was turning in a circle looking at the mountains and stopped when she saw the colors in the sky from the setting sun. "It's beautiful," she said with a huge smile on her face. With both of us standing and looking up at the sunset I said, "Every evening the desert gives us a breathtaking show. Soon there will be artists lined up next to the road with their cameras or painting easels trying to capture the many colors in the sky. Then once the sun goes down it will get so dark you will not be able to see your hand when you extend your arm. But then the beauty of the desert returns again, for when you look up into that darkened sky, you will see every star in the universe, and it will feel like you can reach out and touch every one of them. On some nights there is what we call northern lights, where the whole sky will turn into layers of colors, green, blue, orange, and yellow. And if you sit long enough, you will smell the many desert flowers, you will smell how the air gets heavy with the mixture of dust and dew, and you will hear the many desert creature's miles away making their mating calls." I continued by saying "The Apache have a saying that the Great White Eagle will fan us and protect us with their wings during the day, but with the darkness of night, that is when the Great Spirit can cast dark shadows of fear and evil over all of us through the wings of the evil spirits of reptiles. The desert gives us all this beauty," as I wave my hand above my head, "but you must always respect the dangers that are out there," as I point to the mountains and the open desert. Before Anna could respond, Chief Crowman and Redhorse walked up to us and said they were ready to take us to our quarters at the mission. I said goodnight to Anna and Redhorse and watched as they drove away. Walking with Chief Crowman to his truck, I asked him if we could drive by the burial grounds before we went to the mission, "I just want to take a look and see what it looks like at sunset." He just made a grunting sound and kept walking. I guessed that grunt was his way of saying we'll go to the burial grounds. Everyone on the reservation knows Chief Crowman is a man of few words. But everyone knows when he does talk, it is best you listen, for he was very wise and very observant. So, as we were walking to his truck, I was surprised when he said that he didn't know Redhorse was back on the "reservation." I stopped walking and looked at him hoping to get more information, but he kept on walking. What did he mean? Back on the reservation? I just assumed Redhorse still lived on the reservation. Sometimes Chief Crowman spoke in riddles, and I had a feeling that in his special way, he was trying to tell me something. I made a note to myself to follow up on where Redhorse lives, if not on the reservation, then where.

As I opened the passenger door I was greeted by an avalanche of boxes, papers, soda cans, and just plain old junk that fell out of the truck onto the ground. I forgot how some Indians like to use their vehicles as storage lockers or garbage cans. I looked inside and wondered where was I going to sit, and better yet, did I really want to sit in this truck? I threw the junk that fell out into the bed of the truck, along with a couple of handfuls from inside the truck, and gingerly climbed in. Chief Crowman started driving out of the parking lot and past the guard shack onto the reservation. I had to open the window to get some fresh air because I was starting to feel sick to my stomach from the smell inside the truck. I leaned my head back against the headrest, and it felt as if I was back in time bouncing over the same potholes in a gut-wrenching smelly old truck like I did years ago with Uncle Reymond while staring out the front windshield and looking at the endless brown flatland landscape of the reservation, I forced myself to start thinking of the case. The first thing that was bothering me was what was a big-time war criminal doing in the small town of Isleta, Texas? I kept asking myself that question over and over in my mind when suddenly it came to me. I turned to look at Chief Crowman, who was focused on driving around all the holes in the road, and I said out loud, "It wasn't the town of Isleta Karl Altman was in, he was at the church and the mission." And as if to prove my point I said, "How does a man vanish after the war for almost thirty years? Well, one good way would be by joining a missionary," I said a little louder, causing Chief Crowman to finally look at me. I continued by saying.

"I think he was in a Monastery all those years and somehow was involved with our church at the mission as a monk." Chief Crowman stopped the truck and looked at me and said, "I think you have something there Ryan. The forensic report listed the body as being placed in the ground approximately twenty-five-plus years ago, and noted the body was wrapped in wool-like material, like what a monk would wear." We both sat and looked at each other with a slight grin on our faces, feeling we uncovered a key piece of evidence. "Well, all we have to do now is prove it." Chief Crowman said. "And I think I know how we can," I said. "I bet the mission would have the names of every priest and monk that ever-stepped foot into that church going back hundreds of years." I made a mental note to look at the church history books tonight.

Chief Crowman put the truck in gear and 20 minutes later we drove up and stopped just feet away from the newfound ancient burial grounds. He turned the truck's engine and lights off. I got out and just stood next to the truck to allow my eyes to get accustomed to the darkness. I have always been amazed at how dark it gets in the desert. Tonight, was a cloudy night with no moon, making it even darker than usual. As I stood there, I was thinking Karl Altman was possibly buried in the cover of the night just like this so I was trying to see how difficult it would have been. I turned around and looked in all directions. To my left, I could just make out the silhouette of the Mission and Church even though they were maybe a hundred feet or so away, and to my right, I could just make out three small collapsed storage sheds that were maybe fifty feet away that Mother nature had weathered into a crumbled pile of brick and timbers over the years. To carry a body and a shovel, and then dig a hole in the darkness of night like this, would have been a big undertaking for just one person I thought. So, was there more than one person involved I wondered? And why bury Karl Altman here? Why not in the middle of the desert? Gradually, in the distance I started to see the crime scene tape that I assumed was surrounding the hole in the ground where the body was found. I took one step away from the truck when a strong gust of wind kicked up giving me a chill and caused me to wonder if the Great Spirit was telling me to walk carefully on this Holy Ground. Using my flashlight, I quickly started walking toward where the body of Karl Altman was found. I knew that after all these years I wasn't going to find anything that was going to give me a clue, but I felt I had to look anyway. I immediately noticed it was a shallow hole that was maybe two to three feet deep and maybe five feet long. This made me wonder if the person who buried Altman was in a hurry or was not strong enough to dig a deeper hole or possibly, wanted the body to be found. After looking around for about ten minutes, I turned and paid my respects to the honored ones who were buried in this now sacred burial ground and started back to the truck. As I climbed into the truck, Chief Crowman said, "You know what this means don't you?" I looked at him and said, "Yes I do, some member from the reservation killed and buried Karl Altman here." Chief Crowman shook his head in agreement. Nothing more was said while we drove the short distance to the mission where my room was. Once we were there Chief Crowman said, "When you look into the old priests and monks that worked or visited the mission from those old history books at the Mission, I think you should also look at all the women that would have been at the mission twenty-five years ago, both as nuns and teachers." I looked at him and wondered why he would say to look at the nuns and teachers. What did he know, or better yet what was he trying to tell me? I kept looking at him hoping he would share his thoughts but instead, he just looked at me with a smile on his face and said, "That's what I would do if I were handling the case." Because of the love and respect, I have for him, all I could say was, "Okay, good idea."

As I jumped out of the truck and said good night to Chief Crowman, he said he would pick me up at 6:00 in the morning. I watched him drive away then started walking to the main door into the Mission. I stood and marveled at the fine craftsmanship of the front double doors, I noticed they stood about ten feet tall with rounded tops giving them an imposing and grandiose entrance.

Standing in front of these doors now brought back old memories. I remembered Sister Mary Frances ringing the school bell for us to come in for class. I could still hear her yelling for us to line up according to grade. I turned and looked out onto the field in front of the mission, and remembered how we would play Indian football. There were many days we would go to class all covered in mud and blood. Back then my best friend was Clyde Beckendor, he and I were always competing about who was the fastest runner, who could climb a tree the fastest, and who got the best grades in school. If it involved two, we would always make it a competition. Over the years we shared many laughs and experiences. His mother and my mother were cousins. I heard Clyde died three years ago from a drug overdose. I turned back to the doors, which I know I walked through over a thousand times, but for the life of me, I couldn't remember what it looked like inside. As soon as I opened the door and walked in, I instantly remembered how I always felt this was a haunted house. The foyer or main entrance was a large and dimly lit room with tall ceilings. The walls were covered in a grayish cement-like color and had a rough texture to them. The walls were blank, but for the six black iron sconces, which produced a yellowish light from them. The floors were covered with little green tile squares, which I'm sure the Tiwa woman made. One large iron chandelier hung from the ceiling in the middle of the room. There was a large fireplace that was made with native desert stones on the wall to my left, and except for one old and oversized chair by the fireplace, the room was empty of any furniture. To my right, there was an open hallway leading to the mechanical room, school classrooms, and the library. The wall in front of me had stairs leading to the second floor. I couldn't help but notice the staircase was different from what I remembered. It used to extend into the center of the room but now was flat against the wall, but still had the beautiful dark cherry red banister that went up to the second floor. To me, the staircase just looked out of place. There was nothing about this room that gave me a warm and comfortable feeling. I said to myself the only thing missing was a bad storm and loud cracks of lighting to give this the true haunted house feeling. The second floor was where my room was. Years ago, the priests and monks lived on the second floor, with the third floor being the bell tower. Even with today's outside temperatures going well over 100 degrees, I was amazed at how the foyer was actually cold. I could see burnt logs in the fireplace that someone used to heat up the room with recently. It gave me a feeling of being in my mother's underground fruit cellar which would always be cool and almost cold. It reminded me of my time with the El Paso Sheriff's Dept. Drug Task Force where drug smugglers always kept their drug stash in cool tunnels so the product wouldn't turn to mold from the heat.

 Remembering that Chief Crowman said I was staying in room 212, I headed up the steps to where my room would be. When I reached the second floor I stopped and told myself that the same craftsmen that worked on the walls of the main entry also worked on these hallways. The light fixtures were the same iron wall-mounted sconces, with maybe a 20-watt light bulb giving it a look like flames and giving each fixture just enough light to cast a dim half circle in front of each door on the floor. As I stood there, I could see all the circles on the floor, all the way down the long dark hallway. Walking down the hallway until I found room 212, it dawned on me that Chief Crowman never gave me a room key, but looking at the door, I noticed there was no need for a key because there was no lock, just a door handle. As I opened the door, I reached my hand around into the darkened room and started patting the wall to find the light switch, but nothing. There was no switch on the wall. The room was pitch black, and with the little light coming from the hallway, which was just barely casting light into the room, I carefully took a couple of steps into the room hoping my eyes would get accustomed to the darkness when a cobweb hit my forehead. In a manly way, I swatted it away and immediately realized it was not a cobweb, but a pull string to the ceiling light fixture. After a couple of tries, I finally caught the string and gave it a pull which produced light from a single light bulb dangling from wires from the ceiling in the middle of the room. Problem solved, I proudly said. Now with the light on I could see the rest of the room.

The room was not very large, roughly six feet wide and eight feet long. There were two beds pushed against the left wall with each having a nightstand and a lamp. A wooden cross was hanging above each bed. The wall straight ahead of me had two large windows that looked towards the front of the mission which would allow me to see the newly found burial grounds and the site where Karl Altman was found. On the right side of the room, there were two wooden bookcase-like closets with a desk attached to each, making that wall a desk, closet, desk closet combination. A wooden chair was under each desk. As I turned and closed the door, I noticed a piece of paper taped to the back side of the door, informing me the bathrooms and showers were down the hall. Well, at least the bathrooms weren't outside I told myself. It didn't take me long to get unpacked, and even as tired as I was, I knew I was too excited to go to bed just yet, so I decided to go to the library to look for the books Chief Crowman and I talked about.

As I left my room and started walking down the stairs that would take me to the foyer, my memory was telling me that to get to the library, I had to take the hallway on the far side of the foyer. As I stepped off the last step and stood in front of the fireplace, I couldn't get over how this room felt so cold and empty. I started walking across the room towards the hallway, the only sound I could hear was the loud clacking I was making on the ceramic tile floor, from my Tony Lama western boots. Looking down the semi-darkened hallway, I noticed it looked just like the upstairs hallway, with the same iron light sconces next to each doorway which produced a half circle on the floor and was indicating that there were five doorways down this hallway. Walking down the hallway, I passed doors that were marked Mechanical Room, Conference Room, Classroom A, and Classroom B and finally came to the last door that had no signage on it. My memory was telling me that this was the library. As soon as I opened the door, the smell of the damp and musty old papers told me this definitely was the library. I took a step or two into the room and saw the faint moonlight coming from a red and blue stained-glass window at the far end of the room, giving just enough light to see the dark shadows of a cluttered room.

With my left hand, I started patting the wall next to the door frame for the light switch but after finding no switch I remembered the ceiling pull chain in my room. I swore at myself for not taking my flashlight with me and started swinging my hands above my head until I caught the pull chain and gave it a pull, which illuminated the room from six light bulbs hanging from the ceiling. What I saw next took my breath away. This was not just an ordinary library, but a room filled with thousands of books. I've never seen so many books in my life. There was a thick blanket of cobwebs that was hanging from the ceiling and had started to cover the bookcases. I could see a layer of dust on every flat surface, including the floors. As I made my way into the room, I could see that three of the outer walls were lined with built-in bookcases, all crammed with books. The fourth wall was centered by the large stained-glass window that I saw when I first walked into the room. Under the window, there were two long wooden tables covered with what looked like rolled-up maps and blueprints. There were cardboard boxes filled with more books under the tables. On both sides of the window were bookcases that went up to the ceiling, with one bookcase having a ladder leaning against it. In the middle of the room, I counted seven rows of tall wooden bookcases that were also all packed with books and old ledgers.

I could tell that at one time the books were in a neat and orderly fashion, but over time, everything was just stuffed onto the shelves. In the middle of the room was a large wooden desk that was also stacked with books. The middle drawer of the desk was slightly open as if the last person sitting there was in a hurry and didn't close it. A wooden chair with a broken leg was leaning against the desk, making it look like the chair was declaring itself the last chair standing. I could envision some old monk sitting there at that desk years ago.

While swinging my arms above my head to knock down the cobwebs, I walked to the first row of books, and at random, grabbed a well-worn leather-bound book that looked interesting that had 1865 etched on its cover. As I flipped through the pages, I could tell it was a daily journal of the mission. I read an entry from July 17, 1865, describing a huge fire that destroyed parts of the mission. There were four pages of sketches showing people with buckets of water running towards the fire. The detail of the sketches was amazing. I could almost feel the pain that was shown on the faces of people crying was amazing. Whoever drew these sketches was truly a gifted and talented artist I thought.

I skipped over to the next row of books and found a book that was dated 1886, again this book was a daily journal of the mission, with entries about fighting between the Apache and the United States, with sketches of maps of the area and beautiful drawings of the Apache people. Finally, I found the row of books I was looking for that had daily journals from 1945 through 1980, and I also found the old sign-in books used at the main gate for those years. I stacked the books up to carry and headed for the door feeling excited and hoping these books would have the answers to a lot of questions. Retracing my steps of the hallway and through the foyer and up the stairs, I was finally back in my room.

I laid down on my bed and started reading the books. After two hours I caught myself nodding off to sleep. I got out of bed and went and opened my window to get some fresh evening breeze. I'd been reading boring journal entries like how the deer had eaten most of the corn from the garden and how Mabel the milking cow had stopped producing milk, but I was also able to create a list of all the priests and monks that walked through the doors of the Mission from 1970 to 1980. There were 112 priests and monks. I made the same list for nuns and lay teachers. There were 87 nuns and 48 lay teachers. I have to say, whoever was in charge of keeping records back then, was very accurate and precise.

I was just about to close the book when I noticed an entry on April 12, 1975, about a monk who visited the mission. The entry didn't say who the monk visited or what he did, but he was mentioned in the ledger as a visitor from a monastery in Spain. I set that book down and found the daily sign-in ledger from the main gate for that day and found that someone did sign in at 10:15 am but never signed out. I made a note of that. I was just starting to pack everything up and call it a night when I noticed a copy of the El Paso Gazette newspaper dated September 29, 1978, with the front-page headline IS-LETA MISSION GETS AN UPGRADE. The article goes on about the start of the construction of new classrooms for the school. There was a picture of a man holding a check for one hundred thousand dollars as a gift towards the construction costs. I just put the newspaper in my stack of notes to read later.

Putting all the books down, I started thinking of the events of today. I had to admit, that being back on the reservation was not as bad as I thought it would be. I grabbed the forensic and police reports on Karl Altman and crawled back into bed, not my type of bedtime reading material I said to myself, but I wanted to read it before I fell asleep. It was 11:30 pm.

Day 4: Sunday, February 20, 1994

Who was Karl Altman

> "*A brave man dies but once. A coward dies many times.*"
>
> Apache Chief Johnny Thunderman

By the time I finished reading all the police and forensic reports, I laid there thinking something about this case just didn't feel right to me. I kept asking myself, what was Karl Altman, a wanted World War II war criminal even doing in the small town of Isleta, Texas? And, if someone wanted to hide Karl Altman's body, why bury it in a shallow grave on the reservation and not in the middle of the desert where his body would of never been found? I was having a hard time focusing on the questions and I was fighting to keep my eyes open. I turned my head to look at the clock on the nightstand. I had to rub my eyes to make sure I was actually seeing it right. 4:47 a.m. it told me. Now I knew why I was feeling so tired, I'd been up for over 24 hours. I remembered Chief Crowman telling me he would pick me up at 6:00, so I had just enough time to gather up all the reports, take a shower, and be outside before Chief Crowman arrived. Apaches have this thing about always being on time, so I knew he would not be a minute early or a minute late, but right on time. An hour later, as I anxiously waited outside for Chief Crowman to arrive, I tried to suppress the adrenalin of getting this day started. I stood at the end of the porch and watched the sun peak over the horizon. The air smelled like what my mother always called, "morning fresh". I could feel a faint breeze of wind from the north and the dust from the dry desert sand. Usually, the wind is from the south-southwest, which always blows in the heat and picks up dust from the desert, but this morning the wind was coming from the north, which always means rain. Now on the reservation, we are lucky if we get four inches of rain in a year. So, wind from the north and a rainy day just doesn't happen very often.

    As I stood here on this porch, I remembered the morning when I was thirteen years old. I stood in this very spot with my mother and Redhorse and waited for Chief Crowman to take me to my final test for my "Coming-of-age ceremony. Every young boy starts training for this day at the age of seven. He must first have a sponsor from the community, other than his father. Chief Crowman and Redhorse were my sponsors. Over the years the young boy is taught by his sponsors the Apache language because only English is taught at the mission. The sponsors also teach the young boy how to hunt for food and how to fight.

    When the young warrior-to-be turns thirteen he takes his final test. Apaches call it "Na ii ees". He must walk out into the desert to the mountains called Eagles Peak, some forty miles away, where he must do three things before he can return. He must find a sacred long white tail feather from an eagle that can only be found at Eagles Peak. He must hunt and kill a gray fox and a rattlesnake, both of these will provide food for his journey, and from these, he must return to the mission with the sacred feather, the two eyes from the rattlesnake, and the tail from the gray fox.

As I stood remembering all of this, I had to admit, those were happy times for me, mainly because I knew my mother was proud of me. As I stood there thinking again of my mother, I felt a sudden gust of wind against my face, causing me to think how Apaches have a saying that friendly spirits are always watching and guiding us, and as much as I wanted that gust of wind to be my mother's spirit reaching out to me, my white man's thinking was telling me it was nothing more than the wind blowing.

At exactly 6:00 Chief Crowman drove up and stopped right next to the porch where I was standing, and after I jumped down from the porch and opened the door of the truck, the first thing I noticed was that the Chief had spent time cleaning the inside of the truck of all the junk that was piled in there yesterday. I jumped in and being respectful I didn't mention how clean the truck looked and smelled, nor did Chief Crowman.

We decided our first stop was to go look at Karl Altman's body which has been kept in cold storage since it was discovered at the police station. As I stood over the body, I tried to recall the forensic report that I read earlier. I did notice the small pieces of wool-like material around the neck and chest areas, like what a monk would have worn. I also noticed the bullet hole in the back of the skull. The forensic report also figured this person would have been five foot ten inches tall and showed signs of an old fracture in the right forearm. I looked at Karl Altman's military file and he was listed as being five feet ten inches and having a fracture to his right forearm while in parachute training. Next to the skeleton, there was a very old and worn leather briefcase that was found under the body with the initials P H F etched on it. I carefully opened it and found it was empty. Now, why would Karl Altman be carrying an empty briefcase I asked myself. Was he going to pick something up, or was it empty because the murderer had already removed what was inside of it, and what did PHF stand for? Looking at the briefcase more closely, I thought it was more the latter because I could see the briefcase was discolored and out of shape like something more than sheets of paper had been stored in it for all these years. To me, it looked like a box had been stuffed inside the briefcase years ago, leaving an indentation in the leather. Whatever it was, it was gone now. Walking back to the truck with Chief Crowman, I noticed he kept looking up at the sky, he too noticed the change of wind and knew what it meant. We both jumped into the truck and headed to the trailer. I was hoping Anna had more information about Karl Altman than I did.

When I walked into the trailer, I was surprised and happy to see Redhorse and Anna were already sitting at the table, huddled together with books, folders, and papers scattered around. Looks like she has been busy I thought. Chief Crowman and I walked to Anna's table and sat down, where she started out right away by telling us she received a phone call last night from her father, telling her that we will have two visitors this morning and they have knowledge on Karl Altman. She continued by saying that the Tribal Leaders would not allow them onto the reservation, but they could talk to us here in this trailer. Both men flew into DC last night and were debriefed by the State Department and the FBI. The two were then flown here earlier this morning and they should be here shortly. "These two visitors are aware we are in the early stages of this investigation, and we are to provide them with all the information we have so far, and they supposedly have valuable information to share with us." Looking at her notes to make sure she would pronounce their names correctly she said, "A Monsignor Alessandro Bernardi, who is the Chief Inspector General of the Corps of Gendarmerie", lifting her head to look at us and said, "which is just a fancy name for the Vatican City Police Department, and a Sir Humphrey Denniston of the British Intelligence Department MI6, will be joining us. Both are scheduled to fly out of

DC at 3:00 this afternoon." I told her "It must be something really important if a Chief Inspector General from the Vatican police department and a British Intelligence agent fly halfway around the world to talk to us for a couple of hours about Karl Altman." Anna shrugged her shoulders and said she didn't know anything more than what she just told us. I looked over at Chief Crowman, and we both just looked at each other. I know he was thinking the same as me, and no words were needed.

I was now convinced that there was definitely something more and much bigger about Karl Altman and this case than what we had been told so far.

And as if on cue, we all heard the sound of tires from a car driving on gravel pulling up to the trailer and stopping. "That must be them now," Anna said. We heard the car doors opening and closing and I could hear talking, and then their footsteps as they walked toward the trailer. As I sat and waited for our guests to enter, I thought I would do a quick profile of what I thought a Catholic Monsignor and a British Special Agent might look like. Now, last year I spent ten days in Las Vegas on required classes taught by the FBI on drug smuggling, counterfeiting, and alcohol and gambling. There were other classes offered also, but those were the top three, none of which interested me, and I never had any intention of attending any of them. For me, the first nine days was nothing but drinking, gambling, seeing some shows, and getting very little sleep. On the tenth day, I had to check out of my room by 10:00. My flight home wasn't until 4:00. I had no money left, and I was tired and hungry. So, I went to the last class being offered, a class on profiling suspects. It turned out to be three hours of pure hell. The instructor had this high-pitched voice, with a southern accent that was hard to understand and gave me a piercing headache. I sat in the back of the room where the coffee and donuts were. I ate six donuts and drank as many cups as possible of coffee and I stuffed three additional donuts into my coat pocket for later. Now all was not lost on the class. Between chewing and drinking my coffee, I listened to some of what the instructor said. So, when Anna said a Monsignor from the Vatican and a Sir blah-blah-blah from British Intelligence were coming here, my profiling expertise kicked in and I immediately envisioned the Monsignor to be an 80-year-old man with white hair, wearing his priest robe with a red scarf tied around his waist, with a little red beanie on top of his head. Now the chap from British Intelligence I envisioned to be, middle-aged, stuffy, clumsy looking, and somewhat chubby, carrying an umbrella, and talking with a heavy accent that would be hard for me to understand.

The door opened and well I have to say, I was half correct in my profiling. Which I don't think is so bad, given the depth of my participation in the class. In walked a man whom I swear reminded me of the Pillsbury dough boy. This would be Sir Humphrey Denniston I told myself. He took maybe three steps inside the trailer and stopped. He didn't say anything, he just stood there. My profile on him was right on. I would say he was in his mid-sixties, standing just under six feet and weighing well over three hundred pounds. He was wearing a tight-fitting three-piece checkered or plaid-looking suit with black and white shoes. His face was a windblown reddish color, topped off with thin straight, and somewhat long auburn color hair resting on his shoulders with the traditional English derby hat on top of his head and looking uncomfortable standing in front of us. But the most interesting part of Sir Humphrey Denniston was he was standing there in all his English glory and holding a fancy umbrella, here in the Chihuahua desert, where it doesn't rain but four to five inches a year, which made me wonder, did he think it was going to rain today also? As he wiped his face and forehead of sweat with his white handkerchief, he said in his rich British accent, "Good day-old chaps, my name is Humphrey Denniston." Yep, I nailed it on my profile of the

British Intelligence agent, I said to myself. But what a surprise I got when Monsignor Alessandro Bernardi walked In. He was nothing like I envisioned. For starters he was not 80 but looked to be around thirty-five years old, standing well over six feet tall and weighing a trim two hundred pounds. His short wavy black hair was combed back. He was wearing tan slacks and a blue shirt that he had unbuttoned to the third button. To me, he was looking like he was on his way to a photo shoot for Play Girl magazine. I might have missed it on the profiling of the Monsignor I thought. He definitely looked nothing like the Priests or Monsignors I saw when I was an altar boy at the mission. Looking at Anna, I could tell the Monsignor was having an effect on her because she just sat there staring at him and fumbling with her hair, so I jumped up and walked over to them and introduced myself. After about ten minutes of having small talk and introducing Chief Crowman and Redhorse, Anna finally was able to walk over and introduce herself. We all walked back to the table and sat down, with Monsignor Al sitting to my left and Sir Humphrey sitting to my right. Chief Crowman and Redhorse took the chairs across the table from us while Anna went to her chair at the head of the table. I noticed Anna had unbuttoned the top button on her shirt and I made a mental note to never leave Anna alone with the Monsignor for the sake of his career in the priesthood.

Anna, who remained standing, stood next to her chair and said she would like to present the information she had collected so far on Karl Altman first. No one objected so she led off with, "Once the FBI identified the body as being Karl Altman, a convicted and wanted war criminal, the State Department had no choice but to reach out to European countries and all agencies that monitor wanted war criminals." Anna reached over the table, and using both her hands, she lifted two large and overstuffed folders containing papers and documents, saying "This is just a small sample of what I've received so far from Germany,

Italy, Spain, Great Britain, Poland, Israel, the Vatican, the Polish Holocaust Museum, the Allied Forces Nuremberg Trial Library, the Museum of Sierra, the Israel Holocaust Survivors, the Spanish Historical Society, and the Monastery of Francis de Capillas of Spain. They've all sent information on Karl Altman and they are all pressuring our President to be involved in this case." She set the folders down, picked up her yellow tablet, and continued, "Let me read to you a short version of a Bio on Karl Altman that I created from these folders." She lifted her eyes to look over her reading glasses and said, "You might be surprised, in 1933 Karl Altman owned a small art collector's studio in west Berlin. He was known as an up-and-coming artist, but he also had a bad temper which caused him to be arrested multiple times in previous years on charges ranging from fighting, theft by swindle, home invasion, kidnapping, and possessing stolen property. He spent a total of three years in prison for those crimes. In early 1934, Karl Altman attended his first political rally for a candidate from the Nazi Party named Adolph Hitler. For almost a year he attended every town meeting or rally of Hitler's and finally enrolled in the National Socialist and the Nazi Party by the end of 1934." Anna continued reading from her notes, "By 1936 Karl Altman had worked himself up in the ranks of the Nazi Party. First as a foot soldier and enforcer, then as a squad leader. Altman was known to other party members as one that was a true believer and could be trusted."

"As the years went by, Karl became more active in the Nazi Party, even earning the trust and friendship of Adolph Hitler. In the spring of 1937 when Hitler started constructing his art studio, which he liked to refer to it as the Fuhremuseum, he asked Karl to be the director and art curator. This is the same time of year Hitler was building concentration camps, where he was sending what he called the undesirables, such as homosexuals, blacks, and Jews, to list a few. But before they were shipped to the concentration camps, they were stripped of all their personal possessions, including jewelry, money, and even the gold in their teeth. Their homes were ransacked and anything of value including paintings, sterling, and fine china, was removed and sent to the Fuhremuseum for Hitler's collection. This is known as the start of the Holocaust era that lasted until 1945."

Anna shuffled some papers and continued, "On November 5, 1940, according to the journals sent by the Vatican," as she pointed to the stack of papers on the table, "Adolph Hitler visited the Vatican with a delegation that included Karl Altman. Now, Pope Pius XII never mentions Adolph Hitler in his daily journal, but the Pope does state he enjoyed meeting and talking to Karl Altman and was planning on extending another invite for Karl to visit again." I stood up and walked over to the light switches and turned the lights on. It was getting darker outside from the dark rain clouds and I could hear the rain landing on the roof and thunder rumbling in the distance. Anna made a small comment about the rain, turned her page of notes, and continued to read. "According to documents that we received from the German government", again she pointed to the stack of papers on the table, "Karl Altman was known for his many heists of gold and art. German records show one that happened on November 24th, 1944, during the German occupation of Tunisia, where Altman stole a large amount of gold, diamonds, and ancient artifacts from the government of Algeria. He was almost captured but managed to escape through the port of Annabel. Historians in Spain and France state they have copies of Altman's passport which shows he boarded a Norwegian freighter known as the S.S. Luietz, which was to steam to the island of Corsica in the Mediterranean Sea between France and Italy, and from there steam around to the Baltic Sea to Germany into the Pomeranian Bay. According to German records, the S.S. Luietz, with Karl Altman and the cargo, never arrived in Germany." Anna stopped reading from her notes at that point and walked over to the head of the table and picked up a separate piece of paper and read "U.S. Allies claim to have sunk the S.S. Luietz off the coast of Spain on December 6, 1944, with no survivors or cargo recovered." I looked up at Anna and said, "How can that be? That report is wrong." Anna looked at me, took off her reading glasses, and with a slight smile said, "Nazi hunters from Israel and Spain think Altman and his cargo never boarded the S.S. Luietz, instead they think he boarded a small Spanish fishing boat and sailed to the small island of Tenerife off the coast of Spain, where Spanish dictator Francisco Franco gave Altman a new identity and safe harbor, at which point Karl Altman vanished and was never heard from again." Anna reached for yet another yellow tablet and said, "Let me just mention another curious and mysterious event with Karl Altman's name attached to it that happened in 1941 when the S.S. Minden, a German freighter, was supposedly transporting a full load of gold and stolen artifacts from Rio de Janeiro to Germany. When the ship arrived in Germany, there was no Karl Altman, gold, or artifacts on board, only bales of cotton. Gestapo officials in Rio de Janeiro state they saw the crates of gold and artifacts on the shipping docks and watched as they were loaded onto the S.S. Minden." Anna continued by saying, "In 1946 Allied officials at the Nuremberg trials stated that the Captain of the S.S. Minden in 1941 was also the captain of the S.S. Luietz in 1944, who coincidentally, also disappeared about the same time as Karl Altman did."

Anna took off her reading glasses and said, "These are just two of many unsolved mysteries where Karl Altman was or could have been involved. French and Spanish officials estimate these two heists alone would have a value today of over a billion dollars." She let that sink in and repeated herself again by saying, "You heard that right a billion dollars." After listening for another twenty minutes or so of Anna going over more of her notes on what she had on Karl Altman, Monsignor Al suddenly stood up and politely interrupted Anna in his heavy Italian accent and said, "Excuse me please," and pointing to Sir Humphrey and himself he said, "We were told that time is of the most importance to you on this case, so if you would permit, we would like to share our information that I guarantee will be of great interest to you." How could you refuse a man with that voice I said to myself. Anna just stood there shaking her head yes and turned herself into a bowl of melted Spumoni ice cream and said, "Yes of course" and walked to her chair and sat down, never taking her eyes off the Monsignor, who by now had picked up his notes that were in front of him on the table and started walking around the room. I could tell he was trying to get his thoughts in order on what he was going to say to us. Finally, sliding his fingers through his hair, he turned and looked at all of us, took a deep breath and said, "Now we get to the part of why Sir Humphrey and I are here talking with you. We will be telling you two stories. I will go first and tell you the story of the lost treasures, which I promise is of great importance to you and this case, then Sir Humphrey will follow with his story of who Karl Altman really was." Again, he said, "I promise you that what Sir Humphrey and I have to say will be of great interest to you." Exhaling again, Monsignor Al started his story by saying, "When Pope Pius XII died on October 9 in 1958, Vatican protocol dictated that all personal items of the deceased Pope, like pictures, books, and legal documents be collected and inventoried for historical reasons. It is also required that we prepare a certified financial statement of the Roman Catholic Church as of the date the Pope died, which would include all assets like land, buildings, and bank balances, not only in Rome but in every little town where there is a church or parish, from all over the world. There is also the Vatican Library that we must inventory. It consists of several million volumes of books and thousands of rare and old manuscripts going back to Christ. There is also the complete audit of the Vatican's priceless art collection of sculptures and paintings such as

Raphael and Michelangelo to list a couple, and we publish all of that as the Pope's final Statement of Record. We do this every time a Pope dies. It's a huge undertaking and takes years to complete. We do this as a means of being transparent to the people who support the church and a means of evaluating the leadership and performance of the deceased Pope. This report is then signed by the league of the College of Cardinals as being certified accurate and authentic."

As I was watching and listening to the Monsignor I noticed his hands and arms were always waving in the air. I've heard that Italians have a generic hiccup between their mouth and arms and that if you tied up their hands and arms, their mouth wouldn't work. I was beginning to believe it. But I also picked up a little stress in the Monsignor's actions and voice as if he were hesitant to continue, but after taking another deep breath he continued with, "In 1962, after taking over three years to complete, the Vatican's First Auditor-General, finally released his 6,964-page report of Pope Pius XII final Statement of Record and the financial standing of the Roman Catholic church, listing all the required assets as of October 9, 1958, when Pope Pius XII died. For the first time in the history of the Roman Catholic Church, a final Statement of Record of a deceased Pope was released as a non-certified report", the Monsignor said as he looked at all of us, "meaning the College of Cardinals would not sign off on the report because of an auditors' footnote indicating a number of paintings and one artifact were missing from inventory. The Cardinals immediately ordered a full investigation into the matter." At this point, Monsignor Al thought he needed to drink a whole glass of water to continue. Finally, setting the empty glass down and looking at me and Anna, he continued reading from his notes. "The First Auditor General discovered that six paintings, identification numbers CZ1744, B3998, U2280, B664, J771X, L332XX, and one artifact with identification number JC001 were missing. The footnote goes on to say the six unnamed paintings alone have an estimated value today of over three billion dollars, with the unnamed artifact known as JC001 as being priceless." Monsignor Al looked at all of us and in a serious voice continued with "I'm here to talk to you about the missing artifact, identification number JC001. He continued with, there are less than ten people in the whole world who knows about the missing paintings and less than five people in the whole world who know that JC001 is missing."

"The Pope has given his rare approval for me to talk to you about all of this." Lifting his eyes to look at Anna and me he continued, "To some JC001 is known as the chalice Jesus drank from at the Last Supper, and in other religious communities JC001 is called "The Holy Grail." There was a moment of silence in the room, as that all sank in. The Monsignor continued by saying, "Whatever it is called, it is by far the most valued treasure not only in the Roman Catholic Church but in the whole world, and it's missing." I looked at Chief Crowman and Redhorse to get their reaction, but they just sat there showing no emotion. I don't think they really understood what they just heard. Anna, being the educated scholar in the room, made a gasping sound, and the look on her face told me she understood the religious significance and the historical importance of what she just heard. Now I was raised at the Mission by Jesuit Priests, and among many things, was taught about the Last Supper, but in my wildest dreams, I'd never thought about the chalice still being around today. So, when the Monsignor said it was stolen from the Vatican Museum, that surprised me. Why has it been hidden at the Vatican all these years and never been brought out at a special mass for people to see, like at the Christmas mass or at the Easter mass, I asked myself. Monsignor Al continued talking, "The Vatican has been able to suppress the disappearance of the Golden Chalice for now, saying the Chalice is being restored, but it is feared it will only be a matter of time when the truth comes out that it's actually missing." Monsignor Al stopped and looked at me like he knew of my skepticism and said, "Obviously the history of the chalice is historical, and for over two thousand years armies of historians and treasure hunters have dreamed of and hunted for this mystical religious treasure. That is why we held it in strict security at the Vatican. Ancient historical books tell us stories of how wars have been started from all parts of the world for its ownership. We can start with the stories of the Knights of Templar seizing the Chalice in 1099 from the Temple Mount during the Crusades, to a monk discovering it in a monastery in Leon, Peru in 1144, to Egyptian records from 1928 telling us how archaeologists discovered the tomb of Ramesses ll, who died around 1257, and seeing drawings on the walls of the tomb showing Ramesses holding a chalice believed to be the one and only, the Holy Grail. I can go on and tell you stories of a victorious Russian army who fought for the possession of the Chalice in 1493 during the First Muscovite-Lithuanian war against the Grand Duchy of Lithuania, to the Japanese Empire who also fought for its ownership against a Chinese warlord in 1894. These are just a few of the hundreds of stories of the quests and the many deaths to own the Golden Chalice. One thing is for certain," he said as he looked at everyone in the room, "History has shown us there is a curse on the Chalice and whoever ends up owning the Chalice, death, destruction, and war always seem to follow." I suddenly realized I couldn't move; this story of the Golden Chalice and his tone of voice froze me in my chair. I almost expected to hear a loud crack of thunder and lightning coming from God himself. Monsignor Al continued with, "The story goes that in 1928, a poor farmer from outside of Palermo, Spain, found the Chalice in a cave along with four skeletons. Thinking he found something valuable he brought the Chalice back to his village, where he was told by the elders in the village, that there is a curse on the Chalice and death will come to anyone who owns it. The farmer just laughed saying he was going to keep it and they were all jealous of him because he was going to be very rich.

That night a huge fire destroyed the whole village and killed many people. The farmer blamed himself for the destruction of the village and the deaths of his family and friends. He considered destroying the Chalice, but his wife said he must return it to its rightful owners, the Catholic Church. So, he traveled for six days and returned the Chalice to the Vatican, where Pope Pius, who was aware of the curse on the Chalice, put it in the deepest vault in the Vatican to be locked in secret for eternity." The Monsignor started walking back to his chair, I thought he was done talking, but he suddenly stopped and in a stern voice said, "We thought the Chalice was safely secured in our vault at the Vatican. The Pope and every member of the Vatican, including myself, are extremely embarrassed that this theft happened. I will tell you we know who stole the Chalice, and how it was stolen and now I am here to tell you that we think it's here in Isleta, Texas." I couldn't believe I heard that right. They think the Golden Chalice or the Holy Grail as they call it, is here in Isleta, Texas. I don't think Anna and I moved a muscle or even blinked as we sat looking at each other when we heard that. The Monsignor was now standing by his chair, and was about to sit down, when he said, "Sir Humphrey will now tell you the story about Karl Altman." Both Anna and I were speechless from the story we just heard from the Monsignor. I slowly turned to look at Sir Humphrey, our super spy from British Intelligence, leaving me almost afraid of what he was going to say.

After about a minute of us just watching him sit in his chair, with him not saying anything or even moving, I was starting to wonder if he had fallen asleep. He just sat there with his forearms resting on the table, with his head bent down looking at the piece of paper he had in front of him. Finally, he said in a soft and somewhat quiet voice "I keep asking myself how I tell you the story of Karl Altman. I suppose

I can start by saying he was a man of many hats. He was a war hero. He was a modern-day Robin Hood who helped thousands of innocent people flee Germany, and he was a man from royalty who didn't hide behind the royal crest and fought and gave his life for the freedom of his country. I will tell you that the story of Karl Altman starts on October 9, 1933, which was the day he left for his first undercover assignment in Germany, and the story ends sixty-one years later on February 2nd, 1994, the day you found his body in a shallow grave here in Isleta, Texas. It has taken sixty-one years for his family to finally know the fate of their son. It has taken sixty-one years for the public to finally be able to read all the Top-Secret documents on one Karl Altman, to show how much of a hero he was. It will have taken sixty-one years for Karl Altman to finally come home and to be laid to rest with his family." Sir Humphrey looked at Anna and me for a reaction. Speaking for myself, I still hadn't moved a muscle, and he definitely had my attention. He then continued with, "I was hired forty-three years ago into MI6 as a field agent and the man you know as Karl Altman was already considered a national hero. I am no longer physically able to be a field agent. I'm now the Director of the Agencies Recovery Department. It's a fancy title for a department of just me. My job is to locate missing field agents and see they receive a proper military burial at home. As of today, there are thirty-two cases of missing British agents, of which Karl Altman is one. It was quite a surprise when your FBI requested information on Karl Altman from Interpol. It literally triggered bells to go off all across Europe, causing multiple countries to call your State Department. I know my Prime Minister and my Queen called your State Department, and I've been told the Pope even called. It caused the Monsignor and me to be on the first plane here, and it is with the blessing of the British Royal Family and the Vatican that the Monsignor and I share information with you and your State Department on the Golden Chalice and Karl Altman." He gave us a moment for that to sink in, and then he dropped the big one on us. "Let me next say that whatever information you have, or whatever you think you know about Karl Altman, please disregard all of it, none of it is true. Karl Altman does not, nor ever did exist.

All the information you have on Karl Altman was fabricated by MI6 and British Intelligence. In 1933 we created Karl Altman to be an undercover agent to be sent to Germany to report on Adolph Hitler and the Nazi political movement. The body you found was not Karl Altman, but that of Sir Victor Albert, who is a sixth cousin to King George of the British royal family." Sir Humphrey took a deep breath and slowly exhaled as if to say he was relieved that he got that important information out.

Anna and I looked at each other with a look of, *what did we just hear?* These stories just seem to be getting better and better. First, we have a history lesson on the Golden Chalice going back thousands of years. Then we're told the Chalice was stolen from the Vatican and is possibly here in Isleta, Texas, and now we're told that the body we found in a three-hundred-year-old Indian burial grounds, that we originally identified as convicted World War II war criminal Karl Altman, is actually Sir Victor Albert, a cousin to the King of England, and both of these stories are somehow connected and both ended up in the tiny town of Isleta, Texas, population of fewer than 300 people. You just couldn't make this up, I told myself. I knew there was more to this case than what Anna and I were first told.

Sir Humphrey continued with, "Please allow me to tell you a story of a rebellious, self-centered, spoiled, and out of control twenty-six-year-old rich young man named Victor Albert, the sixth cousin to King George of England. After years of too many parties and arrests that always made the headlines in all the major newspapers, all across Europe, and after being expelled from two Universities in one year,

Victor's family said they finally had enough and told Victor he had two choices, he could continue on with his heavy drinking and partying behavior, but if he did, he would be disowned by his family and lose his inheritance, or he could join the British Army, where the family was hoping they could change the lad. These ultimatums came from his mother and father and King George. After much arguing and fighting with his father, Victor finally agreed to join the British Army, and to everyone's surprise, including even Victor, he excelled and loved his new lifestyle in the Army. Victor did not take the easy route, even though it was available to him, he volunteered for the Parachute Regiment of the First Battalion Special Forces Support Group, and after two years quickly achieved the rank of Staff Sergeant. His military file shows he was well-liked by his men, states he was a fast learner, always the first to volunteer, and he was a true leader, with many of his commanding officers recommending him multiple times for officer's school, all of which he always declined."

Still sitting at the table and feeling comfortable that he now had our full attention after dropping that bomb of information, Sir Humphrey slowly started to lift himself from his chair and shuffled his feet from under the table so he could walk. It was now obvious to me he had a leg problem, and the umbrella was more of a cane or walking stick. Finally able to turn his body from the table, he walked over and stood in front of the living room windows that looked out at the parking lot, which because of the steady down pouring of rain had now turned into a sea of mud. He turned around to face us and continued with, "Victor started to volunteer for undercover missions in Europe and Northern Africa. Even though the First World War had ended just twelve years ago, some politicians in Europe and especially in Germany were secretly meeting and planning for round two of the next war. This was all discussed with Victor, and it was advised he not take any more missions into Europe because he was a member of the

Royal Family." Sir Humphrey slowly walked back to his chair, and with a big sigh, sat down and pulled out a fancy gold cigarette case from his jacket pocket.

After pulling out a cigarette, he tapped it on the case three or four times then placed it between his lips. He fumbled for a lighter in his other coat pocket and finally lit the cigarette, blowing the smoke up toward the ceiling. To me, it was as if I was watching 007 on how to light a cigarette. He finally continued by saying, "In 1933, Germany was the hotbed for espionage in Europe. Not only because of the rise to power of Adolph Hitler but also the spell he had over the German people with his false rhetoric and hate messages. He was becoming more powerful each day. Just about every European country had undercover agents in Germany. Over a period of three months, British Intelligence sent six agents to Berlin, and they all were captured, tortured, and murdered. Some thought there was a mole inside British Intelligence. It was around this time that Victor's persistence finally wore down the upper brass about his desire to be transferred into MI6. After sending five transfer requests and calling in favors from former commanding officers, Victor was finally granted his wish and was transferred into MI6. He went through a six-month Special Forces training refresher course where he additionally learned Morse code, how to ski, and how to fly small aircraft. He was already a skilled marksman and trained in hand-to-hand combat fighting." Exhaling a final puff of smoke from the now finger-pinching stub of a cigarette and rubbing it out in the ashtray, Sir Humphrey continued with, "During the six months of training he was not allowed to speak English, only German. He was trained on how to cook certain German meals and pastries. He even had to acquire a taste for German coffee and their cigarettes. Basically, in those six months, he was retooled to think and act like a German. That's when Victor Albert, the sixth cousin to King George became

Karl Altman. After he had a little plastic surgery, he was issued a new passport and birth certificate. We created school records, criminal records, and former employment records, along with medical and dental records. Some of which you were reading earlier", as he looked at Anna. "We even created an Aunt and Uncle who lived in Berlin, who were to be his handlers and would pass all information from him back to England. When he parachuted into France in early 1934, he hooked up with the French underground and they gave him a safe harbor and travel into Berlin. He purchased an art studio that became very popular with the rich socialites of Berlin. We never knew he had a talent for art, and it turns out he was quite good at it. Victor was also a natural at undercover work. By early 1935 he had become an active member of the Nazi National Socialist movement and eventually met Adolph Hitler. The two of them were drawn to each other with their passion for fine art." Suddenly, there was a rare crack of thunder from outside, causing all of us to look toward the windows. The rain was definitely coming down harder now by the sounds it was making on the roof. There was a slight pause from Sir Humphrey, but finally, he said, "Let's fast forward to the fall of 1939 when Hitler and his Generals were starting to rev up the German war machine with the invasion of Poland. The invasion was quick and decisive, leaving Hitler to predict France and Great Britain would also be as easy, giving huge reassurances that the future looked great for Germany. This was also around the time Hitler unveiled his plans for the construction of his art museum, or as you mentioned earlier, he liked to call it, his Fuhremuseum. Hitler's dream was to have the largest art collection in the world, and his museum would be a place where he could showcase all of his paintings for the world to see. Hitler knew the war would provide huge opportunities for him to seize priceless paintings and artifacts. He became totally consumed and obsessed with his Fuhremuseum, causing Field Marshal Kurt Von Klienster of the German Wehrmacht to state at his Nuremberg trials in 1946, that many military leaders were frustrated and angered with Hitler, they thought he was spending too much time on his Fuhremuseum instead of planning tactics for the war.

The architectural plans for his museum were for it to be the biggest and tallest building in all of Europe. In the early stages of construction, Allied leaders did not believe the stories coming out of Germany, that it was to be an art museum. They believed it to be some kind of military base and plans were being made on how to destroy it. Like many of Hitler's dreams, after five years of planning and construction, the Fuhremuseum was never completed."

Sir Humphrey looked at Anna and said, "Your statements on Karl and Pope Pius II's visits were all correct. Your notes", as Sir Humphrey pointed at Anna, "come from the Vatican daily journals, while my information comes from the Pope's personal daily journals." Sir Humphrey continued with how Adolph Hitler and Karl Altman did meet with Pope Pius XII at the Vatican on November 5th, 1940, and after all the required pleasantries, Hitler got down to why he was really there. He wanted the Vatican to turn over all their paintings and artifacts to the Third Reich and his Fuhremuseum for safekeeping. Pope Pius XII declined, to the annoyance and disappointment of Hitler. Sir Humphrey again looked at Anna and said, "Pope Pius also wrote in his daily journal on that date, that he did not trust Adolph Hitler, but did enjoy meeting and talking to Karl Altman, and was going to invite him back to continue their talks. On November 8th, 1940, an entry in the Pope's daily journal shows an invite was extended to Karl Altman for November 11th, 1940, which was accepted, and the two of them supposedly met for three hours. No details of the meeting are recorded in the Pope's daily journal, nor did Karl forward any information to England about this meeting. Also noted in the November 8th, 1940, entry, Pope Pius writes that two of his personal aids expressed concern about Karl Altman's past criminal history and said it was like bringing the fox into the chicken coop. Pope Pius wrote that if they only knew who Karl Altman really was, they would be surprised! Leaving MI6 to believe that at that time, Pope Pius knew who Karl Altman really was." Sir Humphrey stretched and rubbed his hands on his face and continued, "We don't know why, but it would be three years, September 6th, 1943, before we would find any mention of Karl Altman in Pope Pius II's daily journal again, where he stated the two of them had lunch together."

By now, we had all been sitting and listening to the Monsignor and Sir Humphrey for almost four hours. I for one, had a splitting headache, my back hurt, and I was numb from my waist down to my toes from sitting so long. I was amazed how Sir Humphrey could recall all of the dates and information from memory. I was trying to process the stories told by Sir Humphrey on Karl Altman, a.k.a. Victor Albert, and the history lesson on the Golden Chalice or Holy Grail by Monsignor Al. I kept coming back to, how were these two stories connected and why was Isleta, Texas involved. I had to shake my head and blink my eyes a couple of times to kind of wake myself up. I looked over at Anna and noticed she too was showing signs of wear and tear after sitting for four hours. I tried to make eye contact with her, but she just sat with her head down. I looked around the room, which suddenly I noticed had become dead quiet. Sometime during Sir Humphrey's story, the rain had stopped, so there was no noise from the roof, and I was thankful I didn't hear any snoring coming from Chief Crowman or Redhorse. I noticed Monsignor Al was sitting with his hands folded like he was praying, and I watched Sir Humphrey dig into his coat pocket to find another cigarette and his lighter. I watched him light the cigarette, lean back in his chair, and close his eyes. He seemed either totally exhausted or relieved to get all that information out and on the table.

After a couple of minutes where nobody talked or even moved, Sir Humphrey finally leaned forward in his chair, took another drag from his cigarette, exhaled a cloud of smoke towards the ceiling, and said "Let me tell you about some entries I found the Pope had recorded in his daily journal during the month of February of 1944, which you will find interesting." Sir Humphrey leaned back in his chair and again proceeded to talk from memory. "On February 14th, 1944, Pope Pius made two entries. The first entry was posted at 8:30 a.m. where he wrote, *yesterday my good friend Karl Altman phoned and told me in confidence, of a rumor he heard from a Gestapo General, about the theft of several valuable paintings, artifacts, gold, and cash that supposedly had been stolen from the Vatican Museum. I told Karl that was impossible and there must be a mistake.* The Pope ended the entry with a question mark." Sir Humphrey looked at me and Anna and said, "The question mark made by Pope Pius could imply that he was not aware of any theft. The second entry that day was posted at 3:15 p.m. where the Pope writes, *my heart is heavy with sadness, I have received terrible news that my good friend Cardinal Guido Martini committed the ultimate Catholic sin of suicide earlier this morning.*" Sir Humphrey looked at us and said, "We know Cardinal Martini was a member of the Pope's advisors board and was also the Director of the Vatican's Art Museum. Pope Pius writes in his journal that a suicide note was found, where Cardinal Martini confesses his sins and asks for forgiveness in his time of weakness. Cardinal Martini writes he received a ransom note that morning, notifying him that his 90-year-old mother and 70-year-old sister had been kidnapped and that to save them he was to immediately unlock the Vatican Museum vault and leave it unguarded. Failure to do so would result in their immediate death. Cardinal Martini states that under heavy duress and after praying for forgiveness he unlocked the museum as directed and went back to his room to pray for the safety of his mother and sister." Sir Humphrey stood up, as if to stretch his legs, and continued to say, "At the end of Cardinal Martini's suicide note, he writes that his prayers were not heard. He was notified that his mother and sister were found dead by the Vatican police, in an abandoned warehouse. There has been no further mention in the Pope's daily journal of the rumor of thefts or of the suicide of Cardinal Martini ever again by the Vatican or Pope Pius. Two days later, on February 16th, 1944, Pope Pius wrote in his daily journal that he received a letter of resignation from Petri Hans Frank, Germany's Ambassador to the Vatican, effective immediately, with no explanation given. Four days later on February 20th, 1944, Pope Pius wrote that he was informed that Ambassador Frank had been arrested by Allied forces in Dusseldorf, Germany while trying to flee the country with trunks filled with cash and gold along with crates of priceless paintings. Ambassador Frank supposedly broke down crying and sobbing, pleading for mercy while he was detained, saying he stole the gold and paintings from the Vatican, and he offered all of it to the allied soldiers if they released him." Sir Humphrey gave us a long look and said, "There's good news and bad news on this arrest of Ambassador Frank, the good news is you now know who stole the paintings from the Vatican and how they were stolen. The bad news is the six remaining paintings that are missing, and the Chalice were not in the Ambassador's possession at the time of his arrest."

Sir Humphrey next turned and looked at Anna and me and said, "Now I will tell you how we think the six paintings and the Chalice ended up here in Texas. We believe on February 15th, 1944, the day after Hans Frank stole the items from the Vatican, he divided the stolen articles between himself and his wife. We know Ambassador Hans Frank left Rome by automobile with thirteen of the stolen paintings, along with a pile of cash and gold artifacts. His plans were to drive to Dusseldorf with the intent of meeting Nazi sympathizers who were paid to help him escape from Europe and travel to Spain.

We also know that on the same day, Mrs. Frank, along with her son, left Rome by train with six paintings and the Golden Chalice. After making stops in Denmark and Argentina, she and her son would eventually end up living in Mexico City, Mexico for three years. The 1948 Revolution in Mexico forced Mrs. Frank and her son to move north into the United States, where they settled in the border town of El Paso, Texas, living under her maiden name of Erica Esstler, where the two of them lived until her death in 1959." Sir Humphrey gave a heavy sigh and said "Unfortunately, we lost track of her son Wilhelm, the paintings, and the Chalice at that time." Sir Humphrey gives a loud exhale and shrugs his shoulders and says, "That's all the information the Monsignor and I have pertaining to Karl Altman, Victor Albert, and the stolen Vatican treasures."

Sir Humphrey looked at his watch on his wrist and said, "The Tribal Leaders only granted us four hours to be on the reservation. I suspect a car will be here shortly, so we should rap this up." Looking at us he said, "Are there any questions you have?" I stood up and said, "I don't have any questions, but I do have some information on this case that I would like to share." Looking at both Monsignor Al and Sir Humphrey I said, "What was the first thing you did when you drove onto the reservation this morning?" Both men gave that blank look of I don't know, what? "Well, I will remind you, that you both signed your name in a Tribal sign-in register, listing today's date, the time you arrived, and who you were going to see. And when you leave the reservation this afternoon you will write your departure time in that same register. That is what every person, who's driven, walked, or crawled into this reservation, has done for the past one hundred years. So last night I went to the Mission library, where all the old daily journals and registers are stored. It was my hope that I would find as much information as I could on the Mission and the reservation for the years 1945 to 1980. I did find daily journals going as far back as 1822, and after about three hours of looking, I found what I was hoping to find."

Looking at everyone sitting at the table I half expected someone to say something like good job Ryan, or you're the best Ryan, or show some excitement, but I think they were all as tired as I was, and they just sat there. So, I continued with, "I found the sign-in registers for the years 1945 through 1980 listing every person that would have entered the reservation during those years. This would include every priest, monk, nun, lay teacher, employee, salesperson, or even a member from another Indian community who entered the reservation. I found a couple of interesting items. First, there was an interesting entry on April 12, 1975, when a monk from the Spanish Monastery of St Francis de Capillas, visited the mission. The sign-in register shows the monk signing in at 10:15 a.m. The signature of the monk is not legible, and the register does not list who this person visited, nor is there a sign-out time and signature, which is very strange given the accuracy of all the other entries." Looking at Sir Humphrey and the Monsignor I said, "I believe this monk was our Karl Altman and this is right around the time, according to the forensic reports, when we think he was murdered." I gave a look to everyone to see if they understood or had any questions. When nobody still said anything, I continued with, "I also found a copy of the El Paso Gazette newspaper dated September 29, 1978, where the front-page headline read, ISLETA MISSION GETS AN UPGRADE."

I held the newspaper up so all could see and continued with, "There is a half-page article with two pictures about the start of construction for new classrooms for the school. There was a picture of a man holding a check for one hundred thousand dollars as a gift to the Mission. There was also a picture of two men from the architectural company of Guzman, Garza, and Cabella, from El Reuble, Mexico who would be in charge of the construction. The article is continued on page nine where it is mentioned that a small remodel to the front entryway and a new staircase would also be built to the second floor. There was also a slightly blurred picture of a man standing by the front door of the mission with a baseball cap on and the caption under the picture that says Wilhelm Esstler, a longtime employee since 1960, would be in charge of the carpenters."

I looked over at Sir Humphrey and said, "I believe this is the man you are looking for and is the son of Mrs. Erica Esstler. Last night I also read all the forensic reports and this morning I viewed the body of Victor Albert. The forensic report listed the bullet hole in the back of the victim's head as the cause of death. An old 9-millimeter parabellum cartridge was found close to the body, indicating he was shot by an old German Luger pistol. The victim showed signs of having an old fracture to his right forearm and was five feet ten inches tall, all of which agrees with the forensic reports. The police report notes that when the body was discovered, an empty briefcase was also found under the body with the initials P H F engraved on the briefcase." Again, I looked at Sir Humphrey and Monsignor Al, and again I received no feedback, so I continued with, "I would speculate those initials stood for Petri Hans Frank ." Again, no movement or feedback from either Sir Humphrey or Monsignor Al, so I continued with, "All of this agrees to the information you and Monsignor Al laid out to us this morning, also, while I was in the library, I found the original blueprints for the construction of the classrooms and the remodel of the front entryway and staircase to the second floor. I believe those blueprints will be key to this investigation." Just then we all heard the sound of tires driving up to the trailer. Sir Humphrey looked at me and said, "That must be our ride." We all stood up to say our goodbyes with Sir Humphrey shaking my hand and saying, "I would really appreciate it if you would keep us informed on your investigation. We will be in DC for the next two days and we can be back here within hours if you find anything. After Monsignor Al and Sir Humphrey left and Chief Crowman and Redhorse stepped outside, I sat back down in my chair with total exhaustion. I closed my eyes and started thinking of everything I'd heard this morning. My original orders were to investigate the death of one Karl Altman and to determine how his body ended up buried in an unmarked Indian burial ground. It has now turned into investigating the theft of sacred items stolen from the Vatican some fifty years ago and investigating the death of the cousin to King George of England. Anna came and sat in the chair next to me and said, "What are we going to do next Ryan?" I turned and looked at her and told her I had an idea and asked her if she would call her father tonight and ask that he, Sir Humphrey, and Monsignor Al meet us in the main foyer at the mission tomorrow morning at 9:00. Before she could respond, I stood up and walked out the door. When I got outside, I didn't see Chief Crowman or Redhorse, so I just started walking back to the Mission and went directly to the library and grabbed the blueprints for the remodel of the foyer, then went straight to my room and flopped onto my bed. I needed to get a good night's sleep for tomorrow. Today gave me a major headache. While I was sleeping, I had a vision that the Great Spirit visited me in the form of the White Eagle and told me my thinking was on the right path and my journey was coming to an end. The White Eagle then flew from my window toward the unmarked grave and looked back at me.

Day 5: Monday, February 21, 1994, 9:00 a.m.

The Tunnel with Treasures

> *"A person should be willing to give up all his tomorrows for one today so that he doesn't end up wasting all his days on one tomorrow."*
>
> **Unknown author**

For the past hour, I'd just been lying in bed thinking. I kept tossing and turning. I found myself tapping my chest to the sound of the alarm clock which seemed to be ticking louder and louder. Looking at it I saw that it was 4:00 am. I gave up trying to get any more sleep, so I just got up. By 5:15 I had taken my shower and got dressed. I grabbed the blueprints and literally ran down the steps to the main foyer. I was that eager to get started. I had a plan, and I was anxious to see if my hunch was correct. I knew I would need some tools, like a hammer and crowbar, and I was hoping I would find them in the maintenance room which was next to the foyer. After spending about thirty minutes looking, I finally found the tools I would need. Now as I stood in the foyer with tools and blueprints in hand, I took a deep breath and hoped for the best. I laid the blueprints on the floor to compare them to the actual room. Two things always bothered me about this room. I couldn't understand why it was always cold and drafty, and the layout of the room just didn't look right to me. I thought it was strange that the new stairs were next to the wall and not centered in the room and across from the fireplace like it used to be. And sure enough, now that I'm looking at the blueprints, I could see that the blueprints didn't match the room. According to the blueprints the stairs were again to be built in the center of the room. So, I stood there wondering why the carpenters would not follow the original blueprints and why they would build the stairs against the wall. Now I know there could be many reasons why they did what they did, reasons that I just wouldn't understand, but I couldn't get the feeling out of my head that the stairs were built against the wall to conceal a hidden door that led to a secret tunnel that goes outside. That's what I was hoping. From the first night that I walked into the foyer, I thought it was odd that it was so cold in the foyer and yet it was over a hundred degrees outside.

It made me remember that my mother and I had an underground fruit cellar to store all of our produce and such, and we would go down into the cellar when it got so hot just to cool down. So, it was my thinking, that there was an underground tunnel connected to the foyer which would cause the foyer to be cold and drafty. But after spending about forty minutes going over the staircase and wall inch by inch I didn't find any hidden door that would lead to a tunnel behind the staircase. As I stood there and was almost ready to head back to my room with my tail between my legs, it hit me that the hidden door could be on the other side of the staircase, which would be in the maintenance room. Just then the main door of the Mission opened and in walked Anna and her father with Sir Humphrey, the Monsignor, Chief Crowman, and Redhorse, with Anna yelling she knew they were all early, but they just couldn't wait until 9:00. As we all stood in the middle of the foyer saying our good mornings, they all noticed the blueprints on the floor and the tools in my hand, so I gave them a quick rundown of my idea as they followed me to the maintenance room. As we all stormed into the maintenance room, we found the wall that was on the other side of the staircase, but to our disappointment, the wall was lined with tall metal storage cabinets that were all filled with heavy boxes and tools. "Definitely no door here" I heard Anna say. As I just stood staring at the wall and cabinets, I kept telling myself it had to be here, the door just had to be here. I looked over at Anna and saw a look of disappointment on her face. I saw the Monsignor holding his hands as if he was praying. I walked down the length of the wall, opening each cabinet door as I passed when suddenly, I noticed the last cabinet was a little taller than the others. I then noticed that the cabinet wasn't sitting flat on the floor, it was sitting a good inch off the floor. I could see everyone was watching as I stood in front of the cabinet and gave it a push, causing it to easily move like it was on wheels. Chief Crowman rushed over and gave me a hand and helped me wheel the cabinet away from the wall, and there in front of us was the hidden doorway that I was looking for. The satisfaction and excitement were almost too much for me, causing my knees to feel a little weak, and I was afraid I would drop to the floor.

    It definitely was a rush that I had never felt before. With everyone following me, I slowly walked to the door and turned the door handle, which caused the door to quickly fly open by itself, allowing all of us to feel the cool stale air blowing out of the doorway like a fan. As I leaned into the tunnel, I could see maybe one foot into the tunnel past the doorway. It was pitch black. I couldn't get over the strong breeze of air that was blowing into my face. I remembered seeing a couple of large flashlights on a workbench, so I reached back and grabbed one and then took two steps into the tunnel and stopped. With the flashlight on, I could see that someone had used a pick and shovel to carve out just enough room to walk while being slightly bent over. I noticed that the floor was well-packed and hard as if it had been walked on for many years. I started walking slowly, all the while feeling that strong cool air blowing on me. After taking maybe twenty steps, I could tell somebody was walking behind me, but the tunnel was so tight I couldn't turn around to see who it was. I could just barely get my shoulders through. As spooky as this tunnel was, I was hoping it was Chief Crowman. Now, I know it will be said, that I was a very brave and strong man to be the first one into the tunnel, but truth be told, I was really hoping and praying that I wouldn't see a mouse, a spider, or a bat as I inched my way through that dark and scary tunnel, because I've been told I sound like a girl when I scream. After walking maybe, a hundred feet or so, I suddenly found myself able to stand upright, and with my flashlight, I could see I was in a roughly cut, crude-looking room. I estimated it to be maybe 10' x 10'. On one side of the room, I could see a table with a large used candle on top with two chairs pushed under it. There was also a green tarp covering a large wooden box that was next to the table that also had what looked like an old dirty coat and shovel thrown on top.

On the other side of the room, there looked to be an old army bed cot with a green tarp on top of that also. I was wondering how long it had been since someone had been in this room. I shined my flashlight back into the tunnel and I could see that at the end of my light beam, the tunnel continued to what I assumed to be the grave site. The air seemed to be cleaner and fresher than what it was back by the maintenance room door. As I turned back from the tunnel I could hear someone coming into the room from the tunnel that I had just come from. I was happy to see that it was Chief Crowman, and right behind him was everyone else, including Sir Humphrey, who, with help from Anna entered the room. He had a huge smile on his red face and walked up to me and said, "Ryan, it's been a long time since I've had this much excitement, thank you." Chief Crowman and Anna each had flashlights in their hands making it now easy for all of us to see the room better. I told everyone that I thought the tunnel continued toward the grave site. I saw Chief Crowman and Anna walk over to the old army cot, and I watched as Chief Crowman uncovered it. Then we all heard Anna scream. We all ran over to see what she was screaming about. What we saw was a decomposed body that looked like it had been there for years. Monsignor Al knelt next to the body and started to say what I guessed to be the last rites. After a couple of minutes, he stood up and I said out loud, "If my hunch is correct Monsignor, that will be the missing son of Hans and Erica Frank, Wilhelm Frank Esstler." Sir Humphrey walked over to the body and just looked down at it, not saying anything. I then turned and walked over to the table and said, "And this Monsignor should be what you're looking for, pointing at the wooden box." He looked at me and slowly walked over and lifted the tarp from the wooden box, and I heard a little gasp as he dropped to his knees and started crying.

Saying our Goodbyes

It would take five hours before the tribal police removed the body of Wilhelm Frank Esstler. They took it to the Tribal police station where it would be picked up by the County Medical Examiner's office. The body of Sir Victor Albert would be released to Sir Humphrey and would be allowed to leave the reservation, to be taken home to be buried next to his family and kin. The paintings and Chalice were delivered to Monsignor Al, who had already secured transportation for the return flight to the Vatican for safekeeping.

We were all sitting in the trailer discussing what we had just experienced, and Monsignor Al could not stop thanking me and saying it was a miracle how things turned out. Anna turned to me and asked how I knew about the hidden tunnel. Knowing she wouldn't understand Indian traditions, I told her I had a vision from the Great Spirit. She looked at me and said, "What, you had a vision? What does that mean?" I looked over at both Chief Crowman and Redhorse who were both smiling and shaking their heads. They both knew what I meant. Sir Humphrey stood and said, "Between finding the body of Sir Victor Albert, and finding the paintings and the Golden Chalice, we have indeed found the lost and hidden treasures of World War II."

The body we found in the tunnel was indeed that of Wilhelm Frank Esstler, the son of Hans and Erica Frank. It was estimated he had been lying there for at least 25 years. Death was by a bullet to the back of his head. The six paintings and the Chalice were all intact with no damage to them. It was as if someone had carefully wrapped each picture and covered everything up with the tarp.

I told everyone we still had work to do on this case. Anna spoke up and said, "How can that be? We've identified the body, we've found the missing paintings, and we've found the Golden Chalice. What is left to do?" "Well," I said, " Who killed Sir Victor Albert? Who killed and covered Wilhelm with the tarp, in the tunnel? And someone had to of closed the hidden door in the maintenance room, meaning there is still at least one more person involved." Joseph Friedman spoke up and said, "We accomplished what we were supposed to do. Our allotted time of five days is up and we must leave the reservation today. The Tribal Police can wrap everything else up."

So, we all walked out of the trailer together, and as we all stood at the main gate, I said my goodbyes and safe travels to both Sir Humphrey and Monsignor Al. I told Sir Humphrey that I hoped the body of Victor Albert would find his resting place next to his mother and father, and I told the Monsignor that I hoped there would be no more deaths over the ownership of the Golden Chalice. Next, Anna walked up to me and gave me a big hug, and her father, Joseph Friedman, shook my hand and said, "Another fine job Ryan." He looked at me and said "I want you to take your three weeks' vacation and then I want you to meet me in my office, in DC. You're going to work for me permanently." And before I could answer, they both climbed into their vehicle and drove away. Next, I walked over and said my goodbyes to the Tribal leaders. I could still feel a little tension from them because of my father, but I feel it was a good thing that I did come back, I also knew it was now time for me to leave.

And finally, Chief Crowman and Redhorse came up to me, with Chief Crowman saying "The Tribal leaders have met, and they think it would be best if the Tribal Police close out the rest of the case." I told him I agreed.

The three of us just stood and looked at each other, not knowing what to say. Maybe saying nothing was the best way. I walked up to both and gave them each a big hug and quickly turned and walked back to my car before they could see the tears running down my face.

As I drove out of the parking lot and up to the guard shack I was handed the clipboard to sign out on. I signed my name and wrote Monday, February 21, 1994, 7:10 p.m. As I handed the clipboard back to the guard, I thought of all the times I signed in and out over the years with my mother and Uncle Reymond. I know it sounds strange, but at that moment it was like they were both standing next to me saying goodbye.

As I drove out of the parking lot and turned onto South Red Fox Road, I wondered if I would ever be back here again to sign that clipboard.

Made in the USA
Monee, IL
05 July 2024